Aromatherapy

HEALTH AND BEAUTY CARE WITH
MASSAGE AND ESSENTIAL OILS

MICHELINE ARCIER
Edited by Anne Johnson

BCA

LONDON · NEW YORK · SYDNEY · TORONTO

Project Editor: Isobel Holland
Editor: Anne Johnson
Art Editor: Lisa Tai
Designers: Lisa Tai, Pauline Bayne

Production Controller: Alyssum Ross
Picture Research: Julia Pashley
Illustrations: Pauline Bayne
Special photography: Fiona Pragoff

This edition published 1991 by BCA by arrangement with
Reed Consumer Books, part of Reed International Books,
Michelin House, 81 Fulham Road, London SW3 6RB

Reprinted 1991, 1992

CN 8467

Produced by Mandarin Offset
Printed and bound in Hong Kong

Acknowledgements

The publishers wish to thank the following photographers and
organizations for their kind permission to reproduce their photographs:

Ancient Art & Architecture Collection 11; Mary Evans Picture Library
12; Michael Holford 9; Landscape Only 17; World Press Network
1989, Marie Claire, Martyn Goddard 21.

All other photographs specially commissioned for
Reed Consumer Books and taken by Fiona Pragoff
Stylist for special photography: Elaine Charlesworth
Make up and hair for special photography: Kay Fielding

The publishers would also like to thank the following companies for the
loan of props for photography: British Home Stores, Bodum (UK) Ltd,
Smiths Glassware and China Ltd, Biocosmetics Ltd, Iden Croft
Nurseries, Ian Sanderson Textiles

Contents

Introduction

No-one would deny that aromatherapy is an extremely pleasant therapy, but it is above all a healing art and has powerful effects on both mind and body. It is a holistic therapy, which treats the person not as a collection of unconnected spare parts, but as one unique being.

The key to aromatherapy lies in its dual use of essential oils and massage, thus making full use of two of our most important senses – smell and touch.

THE POWER OF SMELL AND TOUCH

Essential oils are extracted from plants, the healing power of which has been known since time immemorial. They are taken from all possible parts – flowers, leaves, twigs, stalks, resins, even roots – of many different plants, ranging from the ubiquitous rosemary and geranium to the exotic patchouli and myrrh.

Essential oils have many different qualities: they can be relaxing or invigorating, depending on the essence chosen, and are generally strongly antiseptic, antibacterial and disinfectant. As such, they can be used for a great variety of different ailments. They can be applied to the body in many ways: they can be used as inhalations, in compresses, in the bath or, best of all, they can be massaged into the skin.

Massage is the manipulation of the soft tissues and is an ancient method of taking care of the body, both to maintain its appearance and to keep it in a tiptop state of health. The essential oils can therefore be absorbed either through the sense of smell or, if applied to the skin, directly through the pores of the skin and thence into the bloodstream.

AROMATHERAPY

I have taught and practised aromatherapy for the last 30 years. With the help of my assistants – especially that of my head assistant, Judy Warren, whose dedication and loyalty have been a great support to me – I have been able to develop a range of complete treatments to counteract the stresses and strains of modern life, source of so many ills.

The purpose of this book is to give you an insight into aromatherapy as I practise it. It is not intended as a substitute for treatment by a qualified aromatherapist. Some essential oils can be as toxic as others can be beneficial, and it must be strongly emphasized that readers should always check the properties and quality of an essential oil before using it. It should be stressed, too, that aromatherapists are not doctors. If you are in any doubt about your health, it is always wise to seek a medical opinion.

Professionally, I have been greatly influenced by two people. One was Marguerite Maury, Austrian born and married to a French homeopathic doctor in Paris, whom I met at a Beauty Therapy Congress in 1959. She had a magnetic personality. I had always been attracted by a more natural way of life, in a world that was becoming increasingly polluted, and she made me realize that aromatherapy was exactly what I had been looking for.

The other was Dr Jean Valnet, whom I met in 1964. He is the top specialist in aromatherapy in France and he helped me tremendously in understanding the medical background of aromatherapy. I shall always be grateful to him for his considerable knowledge, his terrific sense of humour, and his enormous generosity.

Then, in 1974, I was very fortunate to meet a great philosopher and

spiritual master, Omraam Mikhaël Aïvanhov. His teaching helped me towards a better understanding of the human condition and its spiritual needs. It has enabled me to go deeper into my own work, and to him I owe a great deal.

At present, I am working in my clinic in William Street, London, where I share my time between my clients, training, lecturing, researching and creating new products. My daughter, Marie-Christine, is now managing our establishment. Without her help, dedication and knowledge, I would never have been able to come so far, and this book would not have been written. Our clinic is licensed to treat only women, which explains why this book refers to the client throughout as 'her'.

I am very excited to see the general interest that is now being shown in aromatherapy. I welcome, too, the advances of modern technology, which are constantly proving and confirming the virtue of essential oils.

But aromatherapy could do nothing without its clients. Information and shared communication between aromatherapist and client are perhaps two of the most important factors guiding us on our way forward. It is in this spirit that I offer you this book.

What is aromatherapy?

AROMATHERAPY HAS BEEN USED SUCCESSFULLY FOR GENERATIONS. HERE WE LOOK AT ITS HISTORY, THE VARIOUS PROPERTIES OF ESSENTIAL OILS AND THE DIFFERENT METHODS OF EXTRACTION, AS WELL AS EXAMINING THE MOST COMMON ESSENTIAL OILS IN GREATER DETAIL.

The history of aromatherapy

The history of the use of aromatics stretches back through many ages and many civilizations. Plants have played a part in many cultures over many eras. On closer study of the subject, it soon becomes clear just how great was the knowledge of the ancient civilizations, including that of China, Egypt, India, Arabia and Greece.

THE CHINESE AND EGYPTIANS

Aromatic products were prepared in China centuries before the birth of Christ. In 4500 BC, an emperor of China, called Kiwant Ti, wrote a medical book on his discoveries about the properties of plants. Among them were rhubarb, opium and pomegranate, and what is interesting is that he attributed to each of them the qualities we recognize today.

Egypt was the cradle of the sciences, including medicine, pharmacy, perfumery and cosmetology, all of which were placed under the protection of the god Horus. The tomb of the first ruler of Egypt, King Menes, who founded the city of Memphis in around 3000 BC, was opened in 1897, and revealed the remains of many aromatic products. In 1922, alabaster vases, still fragrant with aromatic preparations, were found in the tomb of Tutankhamen, who ruled from 1361–1352 BC.

Perfumes were used by the Egyptians as offerings to their gods. The temples had a small room in which all the aromatic products were prepared. In the Temple of Edfou, for example, a room was discovered that contained inscriptions detailing the formulas of very expensive perfumes used by the Pharaohs and their families.

The priests were also doctors, and they used all kinds of aromatics, including resins, balms, powders, and so on. These were employed in many different ways, such as in medical preparations, for magical and religious ceremonies, and for embalming the dead.

The statues of the gods were covered in odoriferous oils. Different essences were dedicated to different divinities – such as styrax to Saturn, costus to Mars, myrrh to the Moon, and incense to the Sun. One of the best known perfumes was called Kyphi, which was among those used by the priests. It is said that it was made up of 16 different ingredients, including

Ancient Egyptian women wearing perfume cones. These wax cones were thought to contain herbs and as the wax melted over their wigs, the herbs gave off a sweet aroma.

honey, raisins, myrrh, cinnamon, turpentine, juniper, cardamom and wine, and had a strong, pungent odour.

The Egyptians believed in reincarnation, and therefore wished to keep the body in good condition after death for its journey to its new life. They embalmed their dead with aromatic resins and pure essences. The antiseptic and antibacterial power of the aromatic products used was so great that, in spite of the heat and the passing of time, mummies were found centuries later in a perfect state of conservation. The many deities of the Egyptian religion were usually worshipped under the form of certain animals, such as cats, bulls, lizards and crocodiles, and sacred animals were therefore also mummified after death.

Plants were used in a wide variety of forms and for a wide variety of purposes. The Egyptians knew exactly how to extract aromatic essences from plants. Cedarwood, for example, was heated up in a clay container and the opening covered with strands of wool; the contents were then compressed to obtain the essence. Plants were also macerated in wine and used to make an anesthetic. Many aromatic preparations were made to protect the skin against the heat and sun; cosmetics were used both as an adornment and for their therapeutic properties. For example, an eye unguent, used as eye shadow, also had the effect of protecting the eye against disease. The Pharaohs used to reward their servants by giving them aromatic unguents.

The Hebrews, Greeks and Romans

The Hebrews' knowledge of aromatic perfumes was gained from those of their countrymen who were prisoners of the Egyptians. They used incense and aromatic oils for anointment in religious ceremonies, as well as to fight off evil spirits. They knew, too, all about their therapeutic properties and applied these in medical care.

In Greece, essences were popular not only as perfumes but also as aromatic preparations for the care of the body. They were also prescribed to cure illnesses; Hippocrates attempted to stem the spread of the plague in Athens with aromatic fumigations in the streets.

The Greeks transmitted their knowledge to the Romans. Because of their numerous conquests throughout the world, the Romans had access to many countries producing aromatic essences, and perfumes became widely popular during the rule of Julius Caesar. Baths were in especially great favour, followed by massage with fragrant oils, and places offering these services became popular and important centres of social exchange.

In Nero's palace, some rooms were embellished with ivory plates hiding silver pipes, which were used to spray different kinds of perfume on the assembled guests. These were precursors of our modern sprays and fragrancers. At his wife's funeral, Nero used as much incense as was produced in Arabia in the course of ten years.

THE ARABS

The coming of Christianity and the fall of the Roman Empire saw a decline in the use of perfumes and aromatics. Later on, the Arabs began to use essences, and they perfected the art of distillation. In the 10th century AD, a well-known Arab scholar called Avicenna was credited with the first distillation, though it had, in fact, already been done before his time. The essence of rose was distilled along with that of many other plants, and these extracts were widely used as remedies for various ailments.

The Crusaders learned about essences from the Arabs – particularly the art of distillation as a means of producing quintessences, which were more active than other drugs. They then brought back all this knowledge to their own countries between the 10th and 12th centuries. The invasion of Spain by the Moors also made the exchange of information easier with countries such as France.

Distillation has been practised for centuries.

THE EUROPEANS

In the 15th century, the Italians developed the art of perfumery. When Catherine de' Medici went to France to marry King Henry II, she took with her a perfumer called Cosimo Ruggieri. He was highly proficient in the art of perfumes and the preparation of medicinal remedies to help the Queen. Catherine de' Medici created a vogue for aromatic products, and glove-makers used odoriferous oils and perfumes on their gloves. Ruggieri was also knowledgeable in the use of poisons, with the result that many toxic gloves were sent to the Queen's unfortunate enemies!

The popularity of perfumes spread. In England, Elizabeth I had her cloaks and shoes treated with aromatic oils. Rose water was then very popular and was sprinkled lavishly all over rooms.

In the 17th century, Louis XIV was known to be fond of perfumes. Each day of the week, the court adopted a chosen perfume to please him. Oddly enough, at the end of Louis' life, when he was crippled with disease, he could only bear the smell of orange water.

Many aromatic preparations were sold for a variety of purposes, but most importantly to hide the dreadful smells of unwashed bodies. Aromatic products were also sold as aphrodisiacs, or *philtres d'amour*.

A German pharmacopoeia of 1589 gives the names of 80 essential oils for the treatment of different conditions. At about the same period, lavender essence was prepared for the first time in Provence, southern France. Later on, in the 18th century, two Italian brothers called Farina created one of the first colognes, known as *eau admirable*.

The preparation of flower petals prior to extraction has always been done by hand.

Essences were often used as a means of fighting epidemics of disease, which were quite common in those days. One of the best-known preparations was the 'four thieves' vinegar', made of absinthe, rosemary, lavender, sage, mint, cinnamon, nutmeg, garlic and camphor macerated in vinegar. This was applied all over the body to protect against infection.

The 19th century saw a new scientific knowledge, which meant that more essences were produced synthetically. From these stem the chemical elements used today. There then followed a period of near-complete oblivion of aromatic essences.

MODERN DAY

It is only in this century that there has been a renewed interest in plants and their extracts, and their application in medicine as well as in health and beauty therapy. Aromatherapy is back in favour.

There is a movement among certain doctors towards treating illness with phytotherapy and particularly aromatherapy, especially in Europe and, most particularly, France. Many plant extracts are used in general allopathic medicine, as well as in homeopathic and herbal preparations and in Bach flower remedies. In France, a chemist called R. H. Gattefosse, the author of many books and regarded by many as the father of aromatherapy, studied the properties of essential oils. In the course of his research, he is said to have burned his hand, to have applied some lavender essence, and to have found the healing to be remarkably quick.

Dr Jean Valnet, in Paris, is well known for his invaluable work on aromatherapy. He has trained many in the philosophy of a natural, plant-based medicine working in conjunction with orthodox medicine. He has

written many books, including *The Practice of Aromatherapy*, which I consider to be the bible on the subject.

Austrian-born Madame Marguerite Maury was the first person outside the medical field to study the penetrative power of essential oils through the skin. She based her work on the research of Gattefosse, as well as on her own clinical experience when working with her homeopath husband Dr Maury. She proved that the quick absorption of essential oils through the skin is highly effective. She led the way in the use of essential oils in both beauty therapy and health care, and wrote *The Secret of Life and Youth*.

Some laboratories in Germany and Italy now specialize in the study of essential oils. Aromatherapy is becoming very popular nowadays. Essential oils need to be better understood by both the general public and medical practitioners. The trend for more scientific research, which will make this possible, is only to be welcomed.

The general properties of essential oils

Plants have always played an important role in human affairs. They provide food, clothing and medicines and, by virtue of their odour, they also act on emotions and thoughts to create an atmosphere of wellbeing. Who, for example, can deny the benefits of a walk in the woods, or in lush meadows?

THE EXTRACTION OF ESSENTIAL OILS

Essential oils are extracted from different parts of plants, depending on the oil concerned. For example, jasmine, neroli, and ylang ylang are extracted from flowers; rosemary, lavender, rose, violet, and peppermint from flowers and leaves; geranium, patchouli and petitgrain from leaves and stems; sandalwood from wood; bergamot, orange and tangerine from the rind of fruit; juniper from berries; myrrh, incense and styrax from resin; and vetivert from roots.

THE NATURE OF THE OILS

Essential oils are different from other types of oil in that they do not leave an oily mark on paper, they are highly volatile, and they are mostly lighter than water. It would perhaps be more appropriate to call them essences.

They are generally colourless, though some may be dark red, brownish, blue, green, yellow, or gold. They are acrid, highly flammable, odoriferous and soluble in alcohol, although hardly at all in water.

Mixing essential oils together with a vegetable base oil is a skill which requires training and a great deal of practice.

Essential oils are vital elements. The pure, natural oil is more active than synthetically produced oils, and is less likely to cause adverse reactions. The whole aromatic essence is more powerful than its components: for example, the essential oil of eucalyptus is more powerful than its derivatives eucalyptol.

Chemically, essential oils are made up of a large number of elements, including alcohols, esters, hydrocarbons, aldehydes, ketones, phenols, terpene alcohols, and acids. Most of the elements are known but others have yet to be discovered, and chemists are unable to reconstitute an essential oil with 100 per cent accuracy.

Quality

Many factors can influence the quality of essential oils. These include the country where the plant was grown, the climatic conditions, the way in which the raw material was collected and stored, and the manner in which it is processed. Just as with wines, there are good and bad years for essential oils. Grasse, in the south of France, is the most important centre for the distillation of essential oils.

PROPERTIES

Essential oils are important because of their antibacterial, antimicrobic and antiviral properties. They attack germs, but do not damage tissues.

The odour of essential oils can influence the state of mind. The process by which this works is through the olfactory tract. It is not properly understood exactly how smells are distinguished, but what is known is that tiny odoriferous molecules act on nerve centres, creating a psycho-physiological reaction. An important general property is the fact that essential oils help to reinforce the body's immune system and combat any kind of attack from germs, viruses and microbes.

Unlike many other remedies, essential oils, provided they are correctly stored, always remain active and their power does not diminish with time. The effects of essential oils do not vary greatly according to whether they are taken internally or externally. The ancients knew this; for example, to cure intestinal worms they used garlic both in a drinkable form and in poultices placed on the abdomen.

The main qualities

Some of the main qualities of essential oils are listed below.

General antiseptic: cajuput, eucalyptus, lavender, lemon, niaouli, pine, rosemary, thyme

Antiseptic for respiratory tract: basil, bay, black pepper, cajuput, eucalyptus, incense, lavender, lemon, myrrh, niaouli, pine, styrax, thyme, violet leaves

Antiseptic for digestive tract: basil, bergamot, cajuput, camomile, juniper, lavender, marjoram, myrrh, orange, peppermint, rosemary, sage, thyme

*A haze of mauve lavender growing in fields near Gordes in
southern France.*

Antiseptic for intestinal tract: basil, cajuput, camomile, juniper, lavender,
lemon, niaouli, peppermint, rosemary, thyme
Antiseptic for urinary tract: black pepper, cajuput, cypress, eucalyptus,
juniper, lavender, lemon, myrrh, niaouli, pine, sage, sandalwood, styrax,
thyme, violet leaves
Anti-rheumatic: black pepper, cajuput, camomile, cypress, eucalyptus,
juniper, lavender, lemon, marjoram, niaouli, pine, rosemary, sage, tangerine,
thyme
Good for blood circulation: cypress, geranium, lavender, rosemary, thyme
Good for lymphatic drainage: juniper, rosemary, sandalwood
Good for nervous system: basil, camomile, lavender, lemon, marjoram,
neroli, orange, rose, peppermint, sage, thyme, vetivert, ylang ylang
Good for endocrine system: basil, cajuput, juniper, lavender, rose, sage,
thyme
Helpful in slimming: lemon, rosemary, tangerine, violet leaves
Helpful in problems of menstruation: basil, camomile, juniper, lavender,
myrrh, rose, sage, thyme
Cardiac stimulant: lavender, lemon, rosemary

Highly stimulating: basil, geranium, marjoram, peppermint, rose, rosemary, sage

Uplifting: bay, bergamot, geranium, incense, jasmine, juniper, lavender, orange, patchouli, peppermint, rosemary, tangerine, ylang ylang

Anti-fungal: lavender, patchouli, sage, thyme

Good for disinfecting atmosphere: eucalyptus, geranium, lavender, niaouli

Good for congested, irritated and inflamed skin: camomile, juniper, neroli, sandalwood

Good for Acne vulgaris*:* bay, juniper, lavender, lemon, myrrh, niaouli, styrax, thyme

Good for Acne rosacea*:* camomile, cypress, geranium, juniper, neroli, peppermint, rose, sage, sandalwood

Good for dermatitis: camomile, patchouli, sandalwood

Good for eczema: camomile, geranium, juniper, lavender, neroli, peppermint, sage, sandalwood

Good for psoriasis: cajuput, juniper

Good for wounds and sores: bergamot, cajuput, incense, lavender, lemon, myrrh, niaouli, thyme

Good for warts: basil, lemon, thyme

Good for insect bites: basil, geranium, lavender, rosemary, sage

MEDICAL APPLICATION

Essential oils are used in general pharmacology in many countries, notably France and Switzerland. Remedies are either made up of pure aromatic essences or mixed with other elements.

My own experience is limited to France. Meeting Dr Valnet for the first time, in Paris 25 years ago, opened the door for me to the understanding of the application of essential oils in medical care. In France, essential oils are prescribed by a doctor specializing in aromatherapy. After making a diagnosis, as in any other medical examination, the doctor issues a prescription, composed of a formula of pure essential oil mixed in an alcohol solution. This prescription can be made up in a pharmacy specializing in aromatherapy. The usual recommendation is to take between 10 and 20 drops of the remedy in a glass of lukewarm water, 10 minutes before eating, two or three times a day depending on the prescription. Other preparations of essential oils may take the form of pills, unguents, balms and lotions.

Some aromatherapists recommend self-medication for the internal therapy of essential oils. Excellent as essential oils are, great care must be taken in the light of their current popularity, which has brought with it many unknown sources of production and a danger of chemical adulteration.

I strongly advise people against taking pure essential oils internally, both in my clinic and in my training courses. There are several reasons for this. First, we are not doctors, and only a medically qualified specialist can take the responsibility of assessing a medical condition correctly and prescribing the right remedy. Secondly, the stomach lining could be affected by taking pure essences, whereas medically they are prescribed mixed in an alcohol solution. Thirdly, a lot of experience is required to recognize the quality and purity of essential oils. And lastly, some essential oils can be quite toxic in high dosages, and highly sensitive and allergic people might suffer an adverse reaction to some of their components.

As yet, there is not enough precise information on their properties, good or bad, and the general public is still largely ignorant on this subject.

How Essential Oils are Absorbed

Aromatic essences can be incorporated into a vegetable oil or an alcoholic preparation and applied in many different ways. They can be used as an

A selection of bottled preparations from Micheline Arcier's clinic, including face, body and bath oils.

inhalation, in a compress, in hair care, in the bath, or heated up on a fragrancer to disinfect the atmosphere. They can also be made up into lovely perfumes and they can be massaged into the skin.

The power of essential oils to penetrate the skin is remarkable. They first infiltrate the fatty parts of the skin, and then quickly permeate the different layers to reach the bloodstream. The time it takes for them to be absorbed varies from 20 to 70 minutes.

Many years ago, as part of a laboratory test, a small surface of a guinea pig's head was rubbed with essential oil of lavender. Just 25 minutes later, the essential oil was traced to the animal's kidneys.

CHECKING QUALITY

Colour is an important indicator of quality. In general, be wary of any essential oil that has a watery consistency. Some essential oils change colour with age and oxidation. For example, fresh camomile is blue and turns brown as it ages and oxidizes.

Smell can also be useful, but only to someone who is experienced in the art of recognizing the different odours. Usually acrid, essential oils become highly objectionable when they are not pure.

One piece of equipment that is used by producers, suppliers and researchers to check the quality and purity of essential oils is the chromatograph. This works with the aid of a computer to analyse the various components of the oils.

THE NEGATIVE SIDE

As with everything in life, there is a positive and a negative side to essential oils. They are generally highly beneficial, but some of them can – just like some plants – be toxic.

Sage and rosemary, for example, if used at too high a dosage, can induce epilepsy in very sensitive subjects who have a tendency to it. Marjoram can have a narcotic effect. Peppermint can cause dizziness.

It is important to remember that not all natural products are entirely free of toxicity, just as not all chemical products are toxic. Overdosage or a prolonged and exaggerated use of some essential oils, even when they are pure, can cause toxic reactions.

Some essential oils are highly toxic and should never be used. If in doubt, always consult a trained aromatherapist.

METHODS OF PRODUCTION

The methods of production include distillation, the use of solvents, *enfleurage* and expression.

Distillation

Distillation is done with plants that cannot be damaged by heat. It was one of the first methods of extracting essences from plants, and has been employed for centuries.

Distillation can be done either with water, which is the oldest way, or by steam, which is now the most common method. Sometimes both methods – steam and water – are used together.

A basket laden with rose petals ready for the first stage of extraction. It takes 100kg (220lb) of petals to extract just 50–80g (1³⁄4–2³⁄4oz) of essential oil, making it very expensive.

The principle of distillation by steam is that high pressure steam is passed from a boiler through pipes into a still. The principle of distillation by water is that the still is filled with water which is then brought to the boil and converted into steam. Either way, the steam goes through a vessel containing the plants to be distilled. The steam, now carrying the particles of essential oil, then goes through a cooling system into another container, where the water and oil separate out because of their different densities.

Extraction

This can be done either with the help of solvents or by *enfleurage*.

Extraction with the help of solvents is a complex process, requiring great skill and technological know-how. The most commonly used solvent is petroleum ether.

The first stage of extraction involves a complicated series of extractors producing a mixture of odoriferous materials together with natural plant waxes, known as a concrete. The following stage involves the mixture being washed many times in warm alcohol to produce the most concentrated form of natural perfume, known as an absolute.

In general, it is better not to use essential oils that have been extracted by solvents for therapeutic purposes, as traces of the solvents remain. This method is better suited to products used in perfumery.

Extraction by *enfleurage* is the oldest method of all, and is based on the principle that essences are absorbed by fat.

A wooden frame, known as a chassis, is covered by a glass plate. A slightly warmed grease, such as lard or beef suet, is lightly spread on each side of the glass, leaving a margin all round the edges, and flower petals are then spread lightly on the greased areas. Several chassis are placed in piles so that the flowers are caught between two layers of fat. The flowers are replaced daily and extracts are obtained – with the aid of several washings with alcohol – that are known as the absolutes of *enfleurage*. The fat left afterwards is used by the soap industry.

Because of the great numbers of workers needed for this process, it has become uneconomical. It is only in the south of France, in Grasse, that *enfleurage* is still used today for jasmine, orange flowers and tuberose, the French having a long experience and great skill in the process.

Expression

This is used to extract citrus essences from the peel of lemon, orange, tangerine and bergamot.

The sponge method consists of breaking down the peel by pressing it. The liquid is absorbed by sponges, from which it is then expressed. In recent years, machines have largely replaced the hand process.

The *ecuelle* method is used in the south of Italy. The fruits are rolled around in hollow containers, the walls of which are covered in spikes. The fruits are thus punctured and the liquid flows down into another container, and is then clarified.

HANDLING AND MIXING ESSENTIAL OILS

Essential oils are highly volatile elements, and are very sensitive to both light and oxidization. Their handling therefore requires a lot of care and there are a few points that have to be remembered.

It is essential, first of all, to do the mixing in a well-aired room to avoid being overpowered by the potency of the essential oils, particularly when mixing a large quantity. It is very important to use absolutely clean and dry utensils, as one drop of water would cloud the oils and ruin their quality, while specks of dust would need to be filtered out.

Pure essential oils are best conserved in amber glass (not plastic) bottles, as excessive light destroys their properties and makes the oil turn watery. Always cork bottles immediately after use to prevent both oxidization and contamination of the oil by particles of dirt. Large quantities of essential oils should be decanted into smaller containers, again to avoid oxidization.

Only first-class essential oils and vegetable oils must be used, and it is therefore essential to use a reputable supplier. Price is generally a good indication of quality, as lower-priced mixtures of natural and synthetic essential oils can be produced which are inferior in quality and not suitable for use in aromatherapy.

Mixing is an art for which some people have a gift, while others will never get very good results, no matter how hard they try. Many factors need to be taken into account when mixing. These include the therapeutic potency of the essential oils, their compatibility and the potency of their odour. It is also necessary to make a correct diagnosis of the client's condition and skin in order to use the correct essences at the right strength.

During my training courses, I make students prepare a face oil and a body oil. The recommended percentage of essential oil to vegetable oil is 1–3 per cent for face oil, and 2–5 per cent for body oil. Students make up their oils according to the same formulation, using the same essential oils, vegetable oils and bottles under the same atmospheric conditions. Yet when the finished products are compared, each one is slightly different. It is impossible for two people to reproduce exactly the same thing because each person has different hands and a different electromagnetic field, both of which influence the finished product.

It is possible to learn a great deal in theory, but real expertise can only be gained by regular practice. The art lies not only in mixing essential oils, but also – and just as importantly – in understanding which ones a client needs. The secret is the right oil for the right condition for the right client at the right time. And that can never be a simple matter.

Glossary of essential oils

The properties and quality of essential oils vary depending on the country of origin and the expertise of production. The following list of essential oils, although by no means complete, details those most applicable to my work.

BASIL

Ocimum basilicum

Origins
The name probably comes from the Greek *basileus*, meaning King. Basil has been cultivated in the south of France since the 12th century, while another long-time source is India, where it is regarded as sacred and is consecrated to the Hindu gods Krishna and Vishnu. There are at least 150 varieties of basil in the world. It is a small, odoriferous bush with white flowers.

Essential oil
Steam distillation of the leaves produces a pale green oil smelling slightly of camphor.

Most common uses
- good nerve tonic and natural tranquillizer
- restores harmony in conditions of stress
- helps fight fatigue and encourage mental concentration
- helps the digestive tract, particularly in dyspepsia
- regulates the menstrual cycle
- excellent for colds and coughs
- helps with vertigo and epilepsy
- useful in cases of loss of sense of smell
- can help to shrink warts and soothe insect and snake bites

Used in excess
Can be highly depressant.

BAY

Pimenta racemosa

Origins
A small medium-sized tree, bay grows wild in the West Indies and Venezuela, where it is also cultivated.

Essential oil
Steam distillation of the leaves produces an oil that varies in colour from yellow to dark brown. It has a warm, pungent, spicy smell.

Most common uses
- good general tonic
- strong pulmonary antiseptic, good for colds, influenza, bronchitis, sinusitis and pneumonia
- uplifts people who tend to be depressive or to lack stamina
- good for the hair

BERGAMOT

Citrus bergamia

Origins
Found mainly in southern Italy, the bergamot tree also grows in Morocco and West Africa.

Essential oil
Oil is produced by cold expression from the peel of nearly ripe fruit. It is emerald green in colour, but fades on ageing and on exposure to sunlight. It has a sweet, exotic aroma.

Most common uses
- good for the digestion
- combats intestinal problems, including colic
- combats fever
- uplifting in cases of depression and general fatigue
- restores appetite
- good for hemorrhoids
- good for certain skin conditions, such as wounds, ulcers and scars

Used in excess
Care must be taken not to sunbathe when using any product containing bergamot, as it can provoke problems of skin pigmentation.

BLACK PEPPER

Piper nigrum

Origins
One of the most expensive spices in the world, black pepper has been cultivated for the last 2000 years in southern and south-east India and the Indonesian islands. Today, it is grown in Indonesia, Malaysia and also in Madagascar. Only a small amount of the pepper produced is used to yield essential oil – the main distillation centres being in Europe and the US.

Essential oil
Steam distillation of the dried, crushed, not quite ripe fruit of the pepper vine produces a pale yellow oil that becomes darker and thicker as it gets older. It has a pungent, spicy aroma.

Most common uses
- helps combat fever
- strengthens muscles, which is useful in cases of prolapse
- efficient expectorant, which is particularly helpful in elderly people
- useful antiseptic for the urinary tract and gynecological areas
- good for aches and pains
- good for fatigue and poor muscle tone
- stimulates the digestive tract

CAJUPUT

Melaleuca leucodendron

Origins
The name comes from the Malaysian caju-put, also found in Australia. Sometimes called the swamp tea tree or ti-tree, it has white flowers hanging on a long spike. The leaves are highly aromatic.

Essential oil
Steam distillation of the fresh leaves and buds produces a colourless or pale greenish yellow oil with a strong, clear smell. It creates a sensation of inner purity. As a fragrance, it is a great purifier of the atmosphere.

Most common uses
- powerful antiseptic
- has uplifting effect on mood
- acts on the respiratory tract to help in cases of colds, influenza, sinus trouble, bronchitis, laryngitis, asthma and tuberculosis
- good for digestive difficulties and vomiting
- useful in cases of cystitis and urethritis
- helps in cases of dysentry
- regulates painful periods
- helps neuralgia, along with associated toothache and earache
- good for acne and psoriasis
- beneficial to open wounds and sores
- good for aching limbs and rheumatic conditions
- helps combat intellectual fatigue

CAMOMILE, ROMAN

Anthemis nobilis

Origins
Roman camomile is a very common plant which grows in temperate regions all over Europe.

Essential oil
Steam distillation of dried flowers produces a pale blue oil, which becomes a greenish yellow colour when it ages. It has a warm, fruity aroma. It is recommended in low doses for use on children.

Most common uses
- stimulates and regulates the digestive system
- good for gastric and intestinal ulcers
- calms nervous system
- good for depression, irritability, insomnia, hysteria and anxiety
- helpful in cases of anemia
- eases menopausal problems, such as hot flushes, profuse sweating, aches and pains, and fluid retention
- good for premenstrual syndrome
- relieves neuralgia
- good for several skin conditions including dermatitis, eczema, urticaria, burns, sores, wounds, herpes and psoriasis

CYPRESS

Cupressus sempervirens

Origins
Large evergreen tree found in the south of France, where most of the essential oil is produced, Italy, Corsica, Spain, Portugal and north Africa.

Essential oil
Steam distillation of the leaves, needles and twigs produces an oil that varies from pale yellow to green, with a smell reminiscent of pine needles.

Most common uses
- anti-rheumatic
- beneficial during menopause
- good for circulation and for varicose veins, thread veins and hemorrhoids
- diuretic
- eases coughs

EUCALYPTUS

Eucalyptus globulus

Origins
The eucalyptus is grown in southern Europe, north Africa and Australia. Only 15 of its many varieties are used to make essential oils.

Essential oil
Steam distillation of the leaves and older branches produces a very fluid, pale yellow oil. It purifies the air and can help, in particular, in epidemics of colds and influenza. Eucalyptus is one of the most important essential oils used in pharmacy.

Most common uses
- powerful antiseptic
- soothes respiratory tract and is helpful in coughs and colds, croup, pneumonia, asthma, tuberculosis, bronchitis, sinusitis, and influenza
- useful in cases of cystitis
- reduces temperature in illnesses such as measles, typhus and malaria
- good for neuralgia and migraine headache
- good for rheumatic conditions
- useful in diabetes

GERANIUM

Pelargonium graveolens

Origins
Of the 700 different varieties of geranium, around seven are used to produce essential oils. The most exquisitely scented essential oil is Geranium Bourbon, which is obtained from Réunion, an island in the Indian Ocean that produces half the world's total supply, and Algeria.

Essential oil
Steam distillation of the leaves and stems, gathered before flowering, produces a yellowish green to brown oil with a powerful aroma. It is a joyful, mentally uplifting oil and a great favourite. Its perfume makes it a valuable addition to many therapeutic but otherwise unattractively scented oils.

Most common uses
- has a tonic effect on the entire system
- improves circulation
- diuretic
- helps relieve neuralgia
- useful in cases of diarrhea and gastric enteritis
- helps relieve mastitis
- good for healing wounds and burns
- good for dry eczema and chilblains
- mosquito repellent

JASMINE

Jasminum officinale

Origins
Jasmine is cultivated in many parts of the world, including Iran, India, France, Corsica, Egypt, Italy, Lebanon, China and Morocco.

Essential oil
The oil, which is extracted from the flowers, is a rich ruby colour, with a warm, floral perfume.

Most common uses
- has an uplifting effect on mood and is generally warming
- calming to the nervous system

JUNIPER

Juniperus communis

Origins
Juniper is a small bush found in many parts of the world, including central and southern Europe, north America and Canada.

Essential oil
Steam distillation of ripe, dried fruits and leaves produces a fluid, pale yellow oil, with a woody smell similar to that of pine needles.

Most common uses
- good for digestive problems and stimulates appetite
- strong antiseptic for the urinary tract with powerful diuretic properties and can help clear cystitis, though it should never be used in cases of kidney inflammation
- helpful in diabetes
- good for painful menstruation
- stimulating and uplifting – particularly helpful in cases of weakness
- good for aching limbs and rheumatism
- reinforces the immune system
- excellent for massaging weak muscles
- good for paralytic conditions
- good for several skin conditions, including eczema, acne and psoriasis
- good for healing suppurating wounds

$\mathcal{L}$AVENDER

Lavandula officinalis

Origins
Lavender is a shrubby plant found on the coasts of the Mediterranean, especially the south of France, Italy, Corsica and Yugoslavia.

Essential oil
Steam distillation of the whole plant produces a clear to pale yellow oil with a strong aroma. It is a powerful, energizing tonic that generally produces a state of wellbeing.

Most common uses
- regulates the nervous system
- good for aches, pains and rheumatic conditions
- helps in instances of palpitations, faintness and giddiness
- counteracts stress and relieves fatigue and depression
- highly antiseptic, it combats many types of infection, which may be pulmonary (coughs and colds), digestive (stomach upsets) or urinary (cystitis)
- regulates high blood pressure
- helps in allergic conditions
- can help a number of skin problems, including burns, insect bites, scabies, alopecia, eczema and acne
- regulates scanty periods

Used in excess
Can overstimulate the nervous system.

*L*EMON

Citrus limonum

Origins
The lemon is a small tree cultivated in California, Florida, Israel and Mediterranean countries.

Essential oil
The oil is extracted by expression of the peels, which used to be done by hand but is now done mechanically. The pale yellow citrus oil quickly turns cloudy when exposed to sunlight, and has a sharp, refreshing fragrance. It is an important essential oil because of its many properties.

Most common uses
- highly antiseptic and good for all kinds of infection
- fortifies the nervous system
- cardiac stimulant
- lowers blood pressure
- good for gallstones
- helpful when suffering from ulcers
- diuretic
- purifies the liver
- good for rheumatic conditions
- wards off anemia
- excellent for colds, influenza, sore throats, sinusitis and earache
- useful in intestinal infections, such as diarrhoea
- useful when slimming
- good for hand and nail care
- good for gum diseases, such as gingivitis
- good for several skin conditions, including warts, freckles, wounds and chilblains
- insect repellent

ARJORAM

Origanum majorana

Origins
This is a small plant found in the eastern Mediterranean countries, southern Europe and north Africa.

Essential oil
Steam distillation of the flowers and leaves produces an oil that ranges in colour from pale yellow to rich amber. It has a warm, spicy aroma.

Most common uses
- calms and regulates the nervous system
- good for insomnia, depression and anxiety
- relieves aching limbs and rheumatic conditions
- helps nervous stomach and digestion

Used in excess
Can have a narcotic effect, in high doses.

YRRH

Commiphora myrrha

Origins
Myrrh is a sturdy bush growing in north-east Africa and Arabia. The oldest-known perfume, it was first recorded as long as 3700 years ago. The ancient Egyptians used myrrh for embalming mummies.

Essential oil
Resin flows out of an incision in the stem in small, rounded pear shapes. Steam distillation of crude myrrh produces a thick, pale yellow oil with a warm, spicy aroma.

Most common uses
- has anti-inflammatory action
- good for bronchitis, influenza, laryngitis, chronic catarrh and coughs
- stimulates the digestive tract and is good for poor digestion and flatulence
- has antiseptic action on the urinary tract
- improves menstrual flow
- helps heal wounds
- excellent in skin care

NEROLI

Citrus aurantium

Origins
The main producers are France, Italy and Tunisia but it is also produced in Morocco, Algeria and the Comoro Islands. Neroli is also called neroli bigarade oil or orange flower oil.

Essential oil
Water distillation of the flowers of the bitter orange tree produces a pale yellow oil, which becomes darker as it ages. It has a powerful, exotic, floral perfume, and creates a warm and relaxing atmosphere. After distillation orange flower water is obtained from the remaining water, in which there are still some remnants of the essential oil.

Most common uses
- fortifies the nervous system
- calming for palpitations
- helps insomnia
- relieves anxiety
- good for acne and eczema
- has anti-inflammatory effect

NIAOULI

Melaleuca viridiflora

Origins
The tree grows wild in the French Pacific islands of New Caledonia and in Australia.

Essential oil
Steam distillation of the leaves produces an oil which varies from colourless to greenish yellow. It has an aromatic perfume, reminiscent of camphor.

Most common uses
- helps the respiratory tract and is useful in cases of colds, influenza, pneumonia, sinusitis and catarrh
- antiseptic to urinary tract and good for cystitis
- antiseptic to intestinal tract and helpful in cases of diarrhea
- purifies the atmosphere
- good for rheumatism
- encourages wounds to heal, including small cuts, sores and burns

OLIBANUM (INCENSE)

Boswellia sp.

Origins
This is a small tree growing in north-east Africa and south-east Arabia. Its name means oil of Lebanon. Incision of the bark produces a white resin that resembles teardrops. These are broken off the branches and collected from the ground where they sometimes fall.

Essential oil
Steam distillation of resin produces a pale yellow oil with a rich, peppery smell. It has an excellent purifying effect on the atmosphere.

Most common uses
- good for mastitis
- eases cases of asthma and bronchitis
- has an uplifting effect on mood
- recommended for ulcers
- increases powers of concentration and is conducive to meditation
- stops bleeding and is a good remedy for deep wounds

ORANGE

Citrus aurantium

Origins
The orange tree originated in China. The main producers are Spain, Israel, the US, the West Indies, Papua New Guinea, Sicily and Brazil.

Essential oil
The oil is expressed from the rind of almost ripe fruit from the sweet or bitter orange tree, either mechanically or by hand. It varies in colour from pale yellow to brown, and has a fresh, aromatic smell. It does not keep well, as it oxidizes very quickly.

Most common uses
- general tonic to stimulate the nervous system
- reinforces the immune system
- helpful in the treatment of fevers
- good for constipation
- diuretic
- regulates the digestion
- combats travel sickness
- cleanses the blood
- natural tranquillizer in cases of depression and anxiety
- strengthens muscles
- helps with problems of the mouth, including gum disease and ulcers

PATCHOULI

Pogostemon patchouli

Origins
Patchouli is a fragrant herb found in the Far East and the West Indies.

Essential oil
Steam distillation of the dried leaves produces a thick, dark ruby oil, with a strong, heavy smell. It has an uplifting, soothing, warming influence.

Most common uses
- antiseptic and anti-fungal
- good for all kinds of fever
- good for a number of skin conditions, including scars, acne, eczema, burns, allergies and hemorrhoids

PEPPERMINT

Mentha piperita

Origins
A native of southern Europe, this plant is grown all over the world but now comes mainly from the US.

Essential oil
Steam distillation of partially dried herbs produces a colourless or pale yellow oil that thickens and darkens as it gets older. It has a strong, fresh smell and generally has a refreshing, invigorating effect.

Most common uses
- regulates the nervous system
- good for palpitations
- good for hiccoughs
- relieves asthma
- good for insomnia
- good for migraine
- regulates the digestion and acts as an antiseptic to the bowel
- cleanses the blood
- good mouthwash in cases of gum disease
- good for many skin complaints, such as eczema, dermatitis, over-heated skin, acne, bruises and ulcers

PETITGRAIN

Citrus aurantium

Origins
The main producers are France, Italy and Tunisia. It is also produced in Morocco, Algeria and West Africa.

Essential oil
Steam distillation of the leaves and twigs of the bitter orange tree produces an oil that varies in colour from pale to dark yellow. It has a slightly woody and floral perfume.

Most common uses
- fortifies the nervous system
- calming for palpitations
- good for insomnia
- relieves anxiety

PINE

Pinus sylvestris

Origins
There are many different types of pine tree. *Pinus sylvestris*, one of the varieties used to produce essential oil, grows widely throughout Europe and the USSR, the main distillation centres being in Austria and the USSR.

Essential oil
Steam distillation of pine needles produces a colourless oil with a strong odour reminiscent of balsam.

Most common uses
- powerful antiseptic for the respiratory tract in cases of colds, influenza, pneumonia, asthma, sinusitis, bronchitis and laryngitis
- effective diuretic
- good for cystitis
- good for the gallbladder
- eases rheumatism
- helps prevent epidemics of influenza and other contagious diseases

ROSE

Rosa centifolia (cabbage rose, Moroccan rose)
Rosa damascena (Bulgarian rose, Turkish rose)

Origins
This is a herbaceous shrub that originated in Persia and was gradually introduced to all temperate regions. It has been a favourite of poets throughout the ages. *Rosa centifolia* is cultivated in Morocco, which is the greatest producer, in France, where it was established before the French Revolution, and in Italy. *Rosa damascena*, the deep red, fragrant damask rose, was brought to Europe during the Crusades and is cultivated chiefly in the Valley of Kazenlik in Bulgaria, in the USSR and in Turkey.

Essential oil
The oil is extracted from the flowers and is a dark yellow to deep brownish colour with a warm, floral, spicy aroma. Rose oil is uplifting and is well known for its numerous healing and antibacterial properties.

Most common uses
- helps relieve premenstrual tension
- beneficial for the menopause
- good for depression and mental fatigue
- tones the entire system
- helps alleviate stress
- reputed to have aphrodisiac properties
- good for tired muscles, eczema, thread veins, acne and decongesting the tissues

ROSEMARY

Rosmarinus officinalis

Origins
A shrubby herb, rosemary was considered to be a sacred plant endowed with magic properties in ancient Rome and Greece. Nowadays it is found in the USSR and many Mediterranean countries, including north Africa and Turkey.

Essential oil
Steam distillation of the flowers and leaves produces a colourless or pale yellow oil with a fresh, aromatic perfume.

Most common uses
- general tonic
- cardiac stimulant
- combats rheumatism
- combats fluid retention and is excellent for slimmers
- useful in treatment of problems of the liver and gallbladder
- helpful in treating intestinal upsets
- good for lumbago
- good for sprains and swollen ankles
- improves blood circulation
- good for some skin conditions, such as burns and insect bites
- induces and regulates periods
- has antiseptic action on respiratory tract

Used in excess
If used in too high a dosage can provoke epilepsy and convulsions in prone subjects.

$\int AGE$

Salvia officinalis

Origins
Sage was a sacred herb in olden times. It grows practically anywhere, especially in Mediterranean countries.

Essential oil
Steam distillation of flowers and leaves produces a colourless to pale yellow oil with a strongly herbaceous smell.

Most common uses
- good diuretic and useful when slimming
- helps in rheumatic conditions and good for aches and pains
- general stimulant and regulator of nervous system
- purifies the blood
- alleviates low blood pressure
- regulates menstrual flow
- good for digestive problems
- beneficial in menopause
- recommended in cases of thrush
- helps treat bleeding gums
- helps several skin conditions, such as eczema, alopecia and ulcers

Used in excess
Can overstimulate the nervous system and can cause epileptic fits in prone subjects; use with care.

SANDALWOOD

Santalum album

Origins
A small tree found in India, this is much used in powder form by Hindus in temples and for funeral rites. It is also used for furniture making for its solidity and its resistance to attack by insects.

Essential oil
The tree must be at least 30 years old, when steam distillation of the wood will yield a thick, pale to dark yellow oil with a subtle, very comforting perfume. It is a useful and gentle essential oil.

Most common uses
- has a strong antiseptic effect on the urinary tract, and is therefore particularly good for cystitis
- good for fluid retention
- good for certain skin conditions, such as eczema, abscesses and sores

STYRAX

Liquidambar orientalis

Origins
A medium-sized tree, native to Asia Minor where it grows wild.

Essential oil
Steam distillation of crude styrax balsam produces a viscous liquid, which varies in colour from pale yellow to dark brown. It has a warm, heavy aroma.

Most common uses
- powerful diuretic
- combats pulmonary problems
- good for certain skin conditions, such as sores and abscesses

TANGERINE

Citrus reticulata

Origins
The tangerine tree grows in Florida, Texas and California, where it is the American variety of the East Asian mandarin.

Essential oil
The essential oil is extracted from the peel of the ripe fruit by machine expression. It is a highly vitaminized oil, orange in colour and with a lovely fresh smell.

Most common uses
- good nerve tonic
- helps treat aches and pains
- good for rheumatism
- good for fluid retention
- combats cellulitis
- excellent in pregnancy
- good for children, the weak and the elderly

THYME

Thymus vulgaris

Origins
Thyme has been one of the most widely used aromatic herbs in medicine ever since ancient times. It grows abundantly in Italy, France, Spain, Morocco, Turkey, Israel, the USSR, China and central Europe.

Essential oil
Red thyme oil is obtained by the water and steam distillation of partially dried herbs and is, as its name suggests, reddish brown in colour. It has a powerful spicy smell. White thyme oil is most often the result of adulteration with other essential oils.

Most common uses
- strong general stimulant
- has an antiseptic effect on the respiratory tract and is useful in the treatment of colds, influenza, coughs and whooping cough
- stimulates the digestive process

- has a diuretic effect and is useful in the treatment of problems of the urinary tract
- helps in cases of fatigue, anxiety, depression and insomnia
- helps treat aches and pains
- good for rheumatism
- regulates low blood pressure
- regulates scanty or absent periods
- good for circulation
- combats fluid retention
- good for dental problems
- discourages hair loss
- helps certain skin conditions, such as warts, dermatitis, wounds and burns

VETIVERT

Vetiveria zizanoides

Origins
Vetivert is a wild grass that originated in India. The wild plant does not yield much essential oil, and it is now cultivated in India, West Africa, Brazil, Argentina, Jamaica, Zaire, Haiti and Réunion; these last two are the biggest producers. Its many rootlets mean that it is used as a soil protector in volcanic areas.

Essential oil
The cleaned, dried rootlets are cut into small pieces and soaked in water before being distilled by steam to produce a viscous liquid of a rich amber to dark olive colour. It has a sweet smell reminiscent of roots and wet soil.

Most common uses
- the essential oil of tranquillity, it has a generally calming effect

VIOLET LEAVES

Viola odorata

Origins
This plant was considered sacred in ancient times. Hippocrates recommended it particularly against headaches and eye problems. It grows throughout Europe and Asia, and is cultivated most widely in the south of France, in northern Italy and, more recently, in China.

Essential oil
The essential oil is obtained by extraction of freshly harvested leaves. The oil is a dark green, viscous liquid with a delicate, sweetly floral perfume. It is one of the most expensive essential oils.

Most common uses
- has good antiseptic qualities
- an efficient expectorant of the respiratory tract
- good diuretic
- helpful in cases of fluid retention
- good for slimming
- good for certain skin conditions such as *Acne rosacea*

YLANG YLANG

Cananga odorata

Origins
A native of Indonesia, it is now cultivated in the Comoro Islands, north-west of Madagascar. The trees in this area are pruned to encourage the branches to spread horizontally in order to facilitate gathering the lovely yellow flowers.

Essential oil
Distillation by water, or water and steam, of freshly picked flowers produces a pale yellow oil, with a warm fragrance that creates a wonderfully exotic atmosphere.

Most common uses
- has regulating effect on nervous system
- helps slow down too fast a heartbeat
- helps prevent hyperventilation (overbreathing)
- regulates high blood pressure
- good antiseptic of intestinal tract
- good for impotence in men
- good for frigidity in women
- good for treating fevers
- has an invigorating effect on elderly people
- has an antiseptic effect on the skin
- used in hair care

Aromatherapy techniques

AROMATHERAPY WORKS ON THE NERVOUS SYSTEM AS A WHOLE.
IT HAS A GREAT INFLUENCE ON MOOD AND PRODUCES A
TREMENDOUS FEELING OF RELAXATION.
HERE WE LOOK AT THE VARIOUS TECHNIQUES USED BY THE
AROMATHERAPIST, AS WELL AS AT THE EFFECTS OF TREATMENT.

Massage and its applications

Massage is a healing art. It is the manipulation of the soft tissues of the body. It helps to bring about relaxation, to relieve aches and pains, to encourage the blood circulation, and to assist lymphatic flow.

As well as its undoubted physical effects, massage also engenders a more optimistic outlook on life. It generally has a sedative effect, but can also be very uplifting.

Massage is excellent for the skin, both encouraging it to breathe better and helping the elimination of toxic materials. It also regulates the secretion of the sebaceous glands, and improves the skin's absorption, which means it is better fed. And it speeds up the elimination of dead cells, so improving the quality of the skin.

Its Role in Aromatherapy

I am often asked why I use aromatherapy massage. What makes it different from other types of massage?

Aromatherapy massage is holistic, working mainly on the nervous system as a whole, and including, as part of the same treatment, the head and body. I have never believed in spare part treatment. The human body is one marvellous unit, and must be treated as such. Using pressure points along the spine, aromatherapy massage works on the autonomic nervous system and has an immediate effect of relaxation. Indirectly, it also acts on mood.

On each side of the spine, there is a chain of ganglia (groups of nerve cells) that act as reflex points. Nerve fibres pass through these and group themselves to form plexuses. Nerves radiate out from these plexuses to supply the different organs in the thoracic, abdominal and pelvic cavities. These are responsible for controlling the automatic processes that take place within the body, without any conscious control. The massage movements on these points are based on reflexotherapy.

Many of the massage movements help lymphatic drainage. When blood circulation becomes sluggish, lymph flow slows down. The waste materials are not eliminated properly and many areas become infiltrated. Certain of the aromatherapy movements are based on polarity. Man is a living being, emitting an electromagnetic energy field of many different frequencies, which must be in balance in order to maintain good health. Each part of the body has either a positive or a negative charge, and polarity is the use by therapists of their own electromagnetic field to rebalance that of a client.

Having practised aromatherapy for the last 30 years, I can vouch that this technique has never failed to produce results.

What happens?

The complete treatment lasts about an hour, though the actual massage takes only 35 minutes or so. To lengthen the massage is not recommended, as too much stimulation neutralizes the result.

The massage is always done with face and body oils made up of essential oils and vegetable oils. The products are chosen depending on the condition of the client. It is a good and powerful treatment, much loved by clients. It has to be given with loving care and a great sense of responsibility.

THE EFFECT

The main and immediate effect of aromatherapy massage is relaxation. After the first treatment, a client usually experiences a release of tension, which greatly improves the general condition of both mind and body. Excessive stress causes muscles to contract and even to become locked in a state of spasm. The combination of massage and specific essential oils helps them to release the tension and thus to relax.

There are many factors – stress being the main one – that help to create energy blockages in the body which interfere with its wellbeing. Aromatherapy massage helps to release these.

THE CONSULTATION

Before we undertake any aromatherapy treatment, we explain to our client that she should first have a consultation, lasting a minimum of 30 minutes. This will allow us to record all the information given by her for our files.

But, most importantly, it enables us to assess her medical and social background, which helps us a lot in determining exactly what kind of treatment she should be given and the products we need to use. We have clients of many different ages and from a variety of different backgrounds, and they must be treated accordingly.

The consultation sometimes reveals that aromatherapy treatment would not, in this particular instance, be suitable. It is therefore useful to both the client and the therapist and provides protection for both parties. The information that the client gives is, of course, confidential and is seen only by the therapist who is treating her.

THE TREATMENT

The first treatment that the therapist gives after the initial consultation allows her to verify the information she was given by the client during the consultation. Working on the back, in particular, is like reading a map, and following the different reactions in various reflex zones can give the skilled therapist a good understanding of the client's general state of health.

She also learns a lot about the client from working directly on her body. Is she dealing with a fine or coarse skin? Is it well balanced or dehydrated, mixed or oily? Is it congested? Is the muscle tonicity good? Are the blood and lymphatic circulations working well? Are some nerve points tender? Are there any blockages? Is the spine in good condition? Is the client suffering from a lot of tension? Does the skin turn red when pressure is applied to certain areas? Is the vital flow good or depleted? The answers to these and many more questions tell the therapist a great deal about the client.

Of course, clients differ a great deal and the massage must be tailored to their needs. A young person's system, for example, reacts very quickly, and she therefore needs a shorter, lighter treatment than an older person. An elderly client also needs a short, light treatment, though for different reasons: the elderly person's system has slowed down and has less vitality, and is therefore less able to tolerate a prolonged or deep treatment. Both young and elderly clients also need a low dosage of essential oil.

But even in these two age groups there is some variation that has to be determined by the therapist. The first treatment must always be very light, so as to enable the therapist to find out how the client's system functions and how it reacts. As a general guide, a very toxic body always requires a lighter treatment, otherwise unpleasant reactions can occur, such as fatigue, headaches, aches and pains. The massage liberates toxic elements in the bloodstream, which can cause some discomfort. Until the client's system is purified, the treatment therefore has to remain light. A light, cleansing diet will speed up the process.

The client who is feeling exhausted should be given a light, uplifting treatment, which will usually make her feel lighter and invigorated, and will put her in a happier frame of mind. The most striking result is a deep state of relaxation, the feeling that she is ready to face the world and a glowing complexion.

Our massage movements are usually repeated five times. Most clients feel wonderful after treatment. Any minor discomfort that does occur usually clears up very quickly.

The treatment room

The atmosphere in the treatment room should be harmonious, warm, with subdued light, and imbued with the lovely perfumes of many essential oils. The ambiance of the room and the tranquillity of the therapist herself have an immediate effect on the client.

If she has cold feet, a hot-water bottle will help and is very useful in decontracting the solar plexus, thus speeding up relaxation. Our cubicles are often the last refuge from the hurly burly of the modern world, and we must work hard to preserve this peaceful oasis.

The Role of the Aromatherapist

To be an aromatherapist requires great dedication. Important as it is, it is not enough just to be well trained and to have the required technical knowledge. It is also essential for a therapist to believe in what she is doing and – most importantly in any profession that entails dealing with human beings – to be sympathetic and caring.

As soon as a client arrives, it is important to concentrate completely on her needs in order to assess the situation correctly and to decide which is the best approach for both treatment in the clinic and home care.

Clients are all different. Some are calm, some agitated, some happy, some unhappy, some healthy, some unhealthy. Whatever the situation, the aromatherapist has to adapt herself to it.

Our consulting rooms can be like a stage. Anything can happen, and we must always be in control. A hysterical reaction can be pacified by slow massage of the solar plexus with vetivert, accompanied by some well-chosen, soothing words. An attack of tears is quite common from clients who are under any kind of stress, and is in fact a normal release of tension. The aromatherapist should explain how helpful this release can be to the client. It is often a good idea to play things down a little and even to make a small joke or two. To be a good listener is wonderful, but it is important not to let the verbal flow go on for ever!

A knowledge of psychology is also a great help. Much as the aroma-therapist needs to be caring and understanding, and to listen to her client's problems, it is wise not to become emotionally involved. She needs to be in control. She needs to be firm in order to be able to give help.

The aromatherapist obviously needs to be skilled in her art, and she may find it necessary to explain how the treatment works. A few clear explanations to the client can often help her greatly. The therapist also needs to have a wider understanding of the other natural therapies available, in order to be able to advise her client and to refer her in the right direction when necessary.

Above all, the aromatherapist must have the wisdom to recognize when medical advice should be sought. I always stress to students that we are not doctors. If we are to gain the respect of the medical profession, we must show our professionalism by staying within the limits of our speciality.

Contra-indications

Aromatherapy is a holistic treatment, treating the whole person, and there are therefore times when it is not advisable. Contra-indications include all the following conditions:

- ✗ the post-operative state
- ✗ advanced heart conditions
- ✗ advanced asthmatic conditions

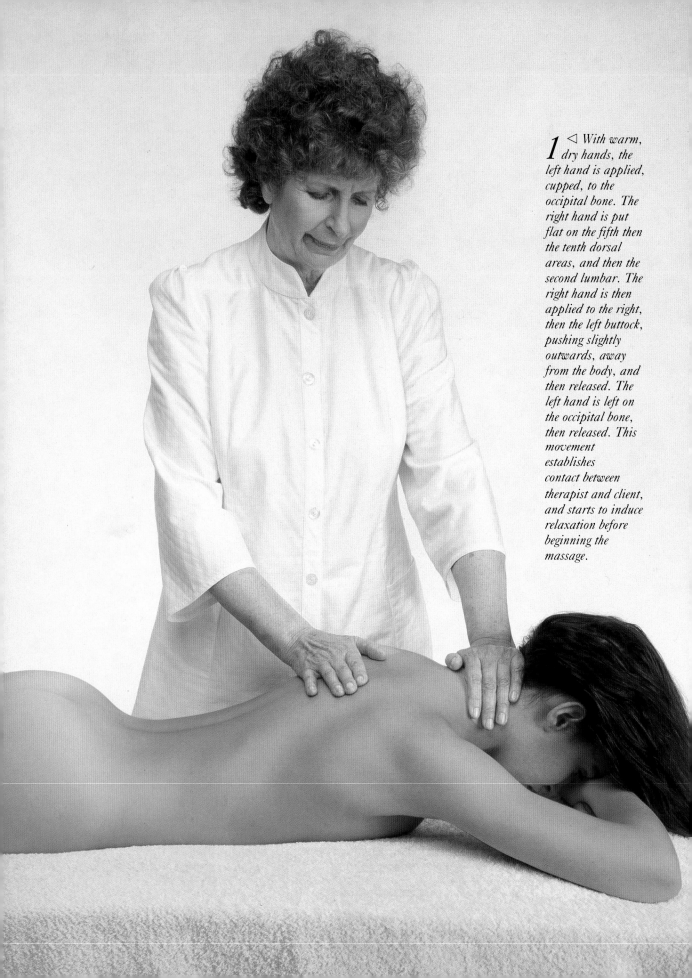

1 ◁ *With warm, dry hands, the left hand is applied, cupped, to the occipital bone. The right hand is put flat on the fifth then the tenth dorsal areas, and then the second lumbar. The right hand is then applied to the right, then the left buttock, pushing slightly outwards, away from the body, and then released. The left hand is left on the occipital bone, then released. This movement establishes contact between therapist and client, and starts to induce relaxation before beginning the massage.*

✗ advanced cancer cases

✗ advanced varicose veins

✗ any acute condition.

A doctor's written consent should first be obtained before treating any of the above conditions. The wisest recommendation we can give is: if in doubt, don't.

HOME CARE

Having given the client a consultation and treatment, it is now possible to make an overall assessment of the situation. On the basis of this, the client can be given a few simple recommendations, including advice on diet, exercise and so on – and, most importantly, a programme of home care, using face, body and bath oils, with which she can continue the work that was started at the clinic.

These products are not only good for the skin but also help with many different conditions. The way in which to use them is detailed in Skin Care (see pages 105–116).

Aromatherapy massage

These are the main massage movements used by the aromatherapist as part of a client's treatment in the clinic. The massage movements are usually repeated five times. The atmosphere in the treatment room is always restful to enable the client to relax completely and benefit from the massage.

2 △ *Pressure is applied to points along the occipital bone to alleviate muscle contractions and fluid infiltrations.*

3 △ *The fingers slide along the cranial bone up to the tip of the head, in order to release the energy flow from the body.*

4 ▷ *The body oil is applied with a movement of* effleurage. *Using both thumbs, pressure is applied on either side of the spine to stimulate the nerve influx. The same movement is then repeated but using a sliding motion to stimulate currents along the spine.* Effleurage *is any sliding movement that is soothing to the skin. It is done throughout the massage between movements to give continuity to the massage.*

5 ▽ *The tissue is loosened all over the back to help remove waste materials, while at the same time speeding up blood and lymph flow.*

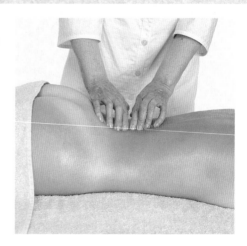

6 *a)b)c)* ▷ *The nervous influx is liberated by a sequence of sliding movements of the fingers away from the spine, working on each side of the spine alternately and moving from the buttocks to the shoulders.*

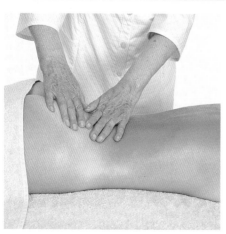

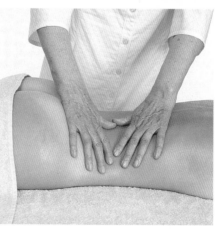

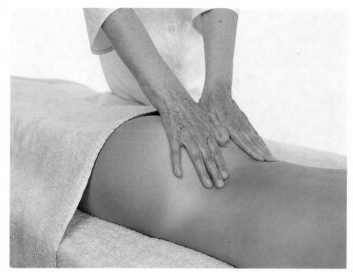

7 ◁ *With the hands on the hip and buttock region, a gentle movement of* effleurage *helps to spread oil over the whole area.*

8 ▽ *A deep circular movement of the thumbs is used, working from the coccygeal area to the hip bone. This helps to release waste materials and relieve any congestive state.*

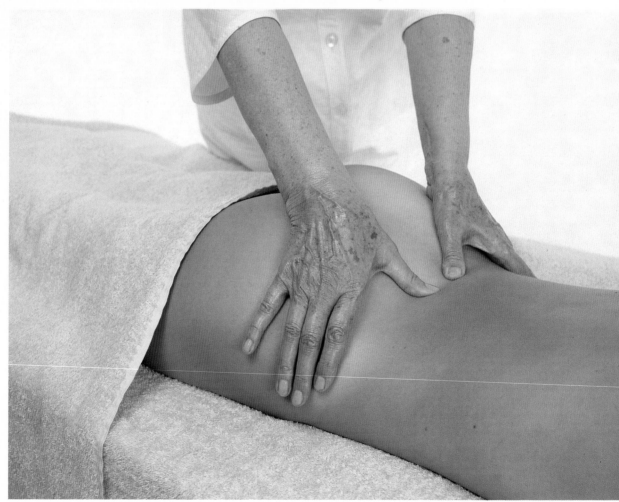

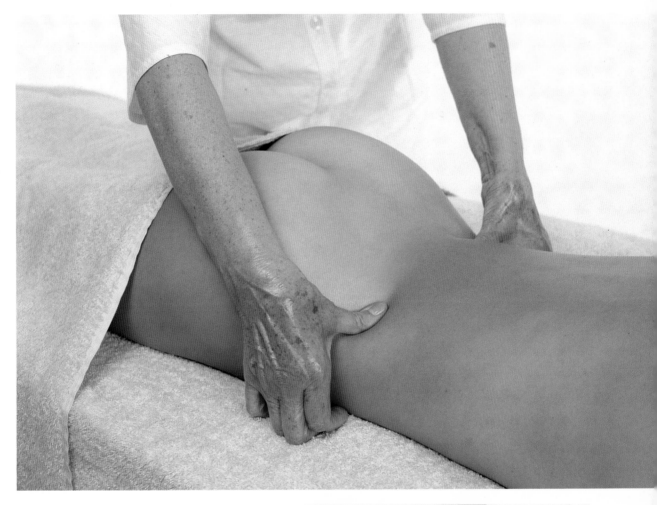

9 △ *A deep sliding movement of the thumbs all over the buttock area helps to speed up the circulation and improve lymphatic drainage.*

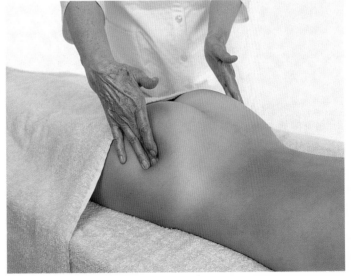

10 ▷ *Pressure is applied with the middle finger on the hip plexus and the flat of the hand then rests over the same area to release nerve tension.*

11 ▷ *Both hands are placed flat on the lumbar region and a slow* effleurage *movement is given on the kidney area.*

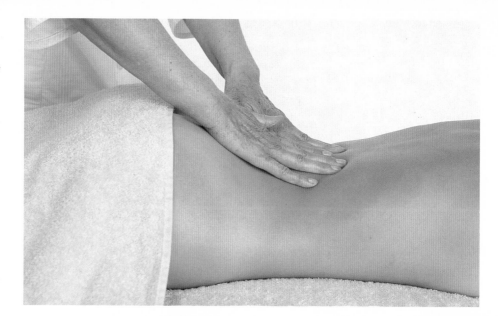

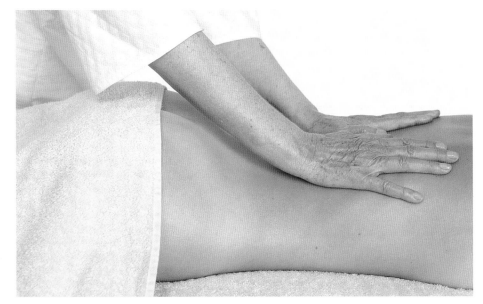

12 ◁ *With a fanning movement, the kidney area is well massaged from the centre to the sides of the body.*

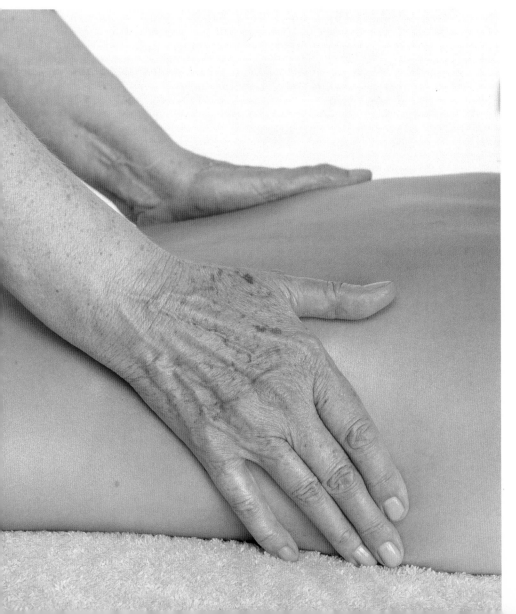

13 ◁ *Massage over the kidney area helps to eliminate and disperse fluid retention and improves lymphatic drainage.*

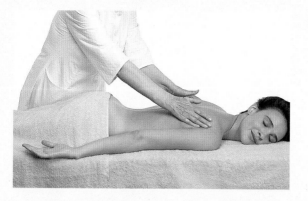

14 ◁ ◁ *With the client's arms on the couch, the hands slide up gently from the lumbar area.*

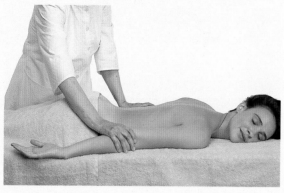

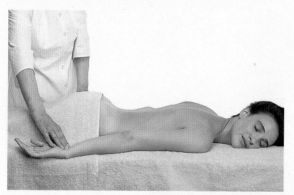

15 *a)b)c)* ◁ *First, pressure is applied to the lymph point in the shoulder area. The hands then slide along the arm, working on the pressure points inside the elbow and on the wrist and palm of the hand in order to stimulate lymph flow.*

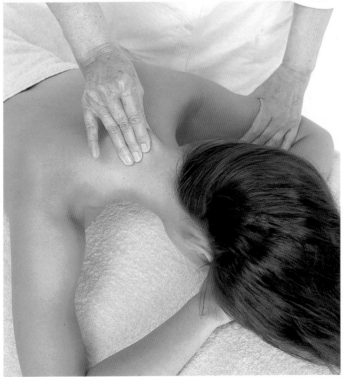

16 ◁ ◁ *The hands are placed on both shoulders to give a movement of* petrissage, *which helps to release tension.* Petrissage *works deeply on the muscles by lifting them up, and then pressing and releasing them alternately.*

17 ◁ *Concentrating on one shoulder at a time, both hands are used alternately to give a deep petrissage movement, which releases tension.*

18 ◁ *With one hand on each shoulder a soothing movement completes the release of tension in the muscles.*

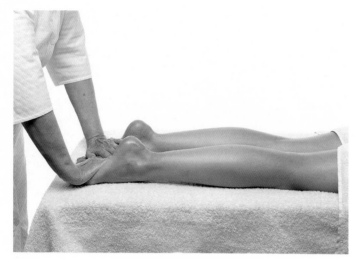

19 ◁ *After applying oil to both legs with a movement of* effleurage, *the hands are then placed flat on the soles of the feet and held there for two counts.*

20 ▷ *The hands are cupped on the ankles, where there is an important energy centre, and held there for two counts.*

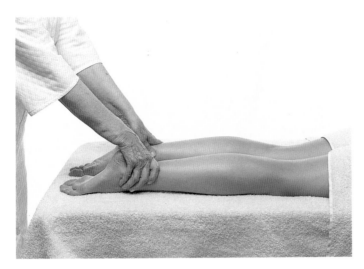

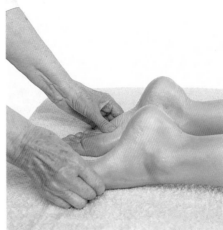

21 ◁ *The hands slide from the ankles to the back of the knees and are held there for two counts. They then slide up to the top of the thighs. This movement helps the release of tension and improves both lymph flow and blood circulation.*

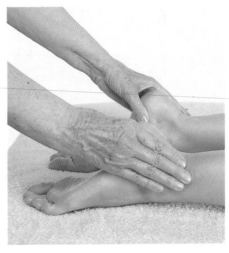

22 a)b) △ *Circular movements with the thumbs on the soles and then the heels of the feet stimulate the reflex points which, in turn, stimulate the corresponding organs in the body.*

23. ▷ *The client turns over on to her back. With clean, dry hands, work begins on the head. Pressure is applied to points over the top of the head along the cranial fissure to contact the endocrine points and stimulate the whole system.*

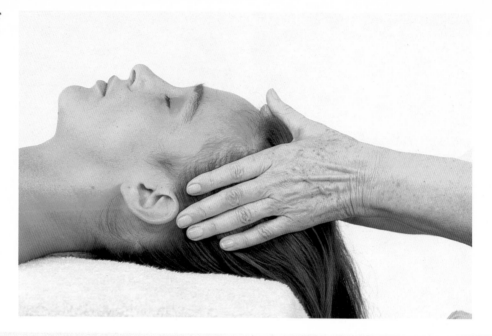

24 ◁ *Circular movements with the fingers all over the head loosen the scalp. This helps blood circulation, encourages hair growth and releases tension in the muscles of the head.*

25 ◁ *The hands are drawn through to the ends of the hair to disperse energy flow.*

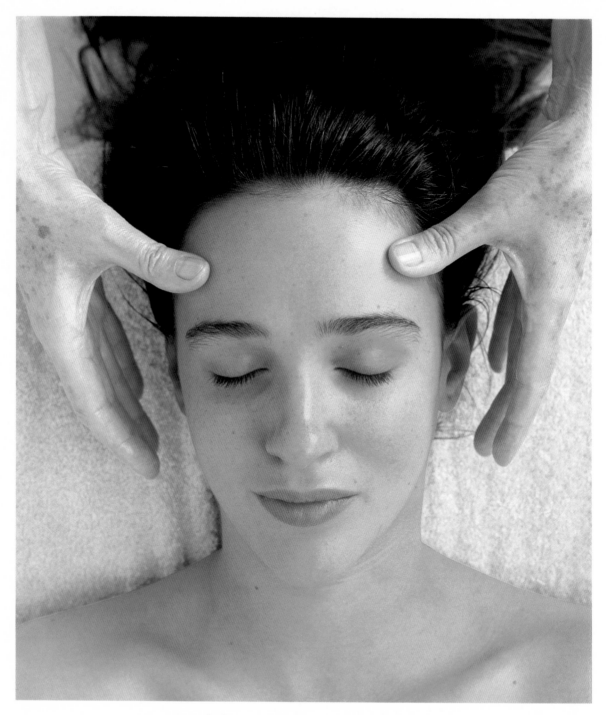

26 △ *Oil is applied all over the face and neck with a movement of* effleurage. *Pressure points all over the forehead stimulate the energy centre and release tension.*

27 △ *Deep pressure is applied on the corrugator muscle, which is a small muscle on each side of the root of the nose, sliding up to the hair line. This releases tension and soothes the frowning muscle.*

28 △ *Soothing movements, sliding the hands alternately over the forehead, have a very relaxing effect.*

29 △ *Movements on the muscles round the eyes and eyelids improve blood circulation and relax eye strain.*

30 △ *The corrugator muscle is lifted up and pressure applied inside the bone near the eye to relieve eye strain and sinus problems.*

31 ◁ *The fingers slide flat from the nose outwards over the cheek bone towards the temple, to encourage sinus drainage.*

32 ◁ *Using the tips of the fingers and with the hands slightly cupped, light pressure is applied to the cheek bone, from the corner of the nose to the side of the face. This helps to release tension.*

33 ◁ *To encourage lymphatic drainage, pressure is applied with the two hands from the corner of the nose over the lymphatic points of the face, right up to the ear area.*

34 ◁ *With the two hands over the face, a vibrating movement stimulates the muscles and therefore helps their tonicity.*

35 ◁ *The contours of the face are massaged with the fingers placed under the jaw bone and the thumbs working in a circular movement from the chin to the end of the jaw bone. This helps muscle tonicity and relieves infiltrations of fluid and fat.*

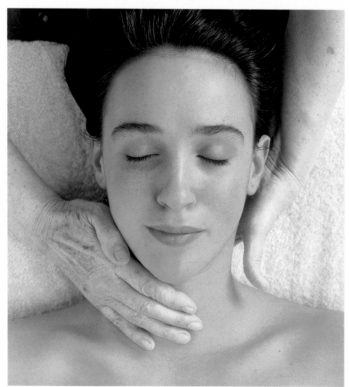

36 ◁ *The hands slide from one side of the neck to the other, to improve muscle tonicity and to tone the quality of the skin.*

37 ▷ *Soothing movements are done with both hands on each side of the neck area to improve skin tone.*

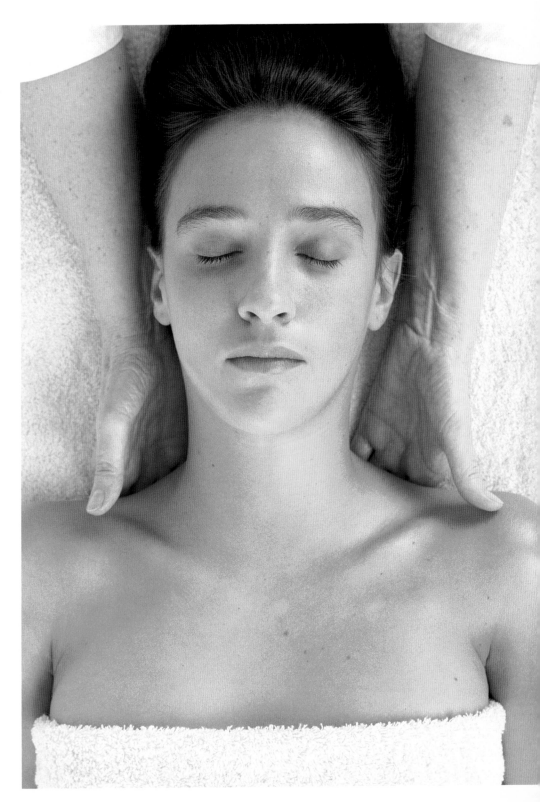

38 ◁ ◁ *The hands slide down to the breast area to stimulate lymphatic drainage.*

39 ◁ *Pressure is applied round the shoulders to help release tension.*

40 ◁ ◁ *Both hands are placed flat at the back of the neck to help release tension.*

41 ◁ *A soothing movement is applied to the cranium working in an upward direction.*

42 ▷ *A circular movement of the fingers on the trapezius muscle in the shoulder area decontracts and relaxes the muscle.*

43 ◁ *A deep movement of* petrissage *on the* shoulders *decontracts the muscles, releases tension and disperses localized infiltration of fat and fluid.*

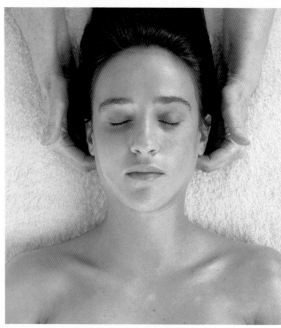

44 ◁ *The fingers are cupped against the occiptal bone and the neck is slightly stretched to release tension.*

45 ◁ *With the hands cupped under the back of the neck, they gently lift and vibrate. This action is very relaxing to the client.*

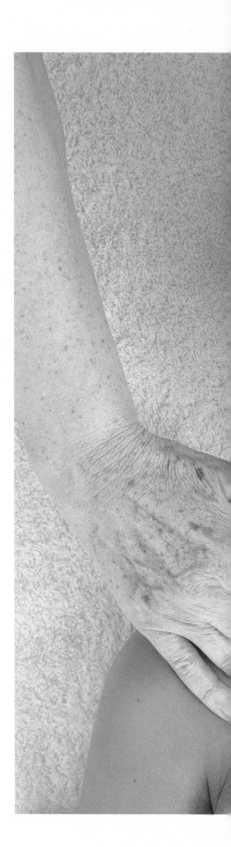

46 ◁ Massage is given below the clavicle, around the shoulders, up the sides of the neck and along the side of the head to stimulate lymphatic drainage.

47 △ *An anti-clockwise movement on the solar plexus, using the right hand and resting the left hand on the client's arm, releases tension.*

48 ▷ *Both hands are placed on either side of the diaphragm and a gentle sliding downward movement is used to liberate tension.*

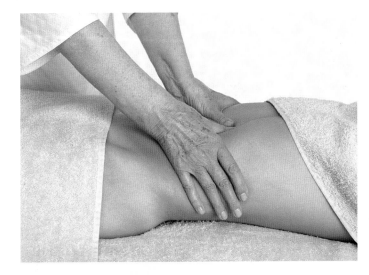

49 ▷ *Sliding the hand down along the ribs liberates the diaphragm. This improves breathing and helps relaxation.*

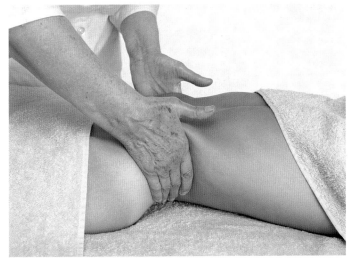

50 ▷ *The right hand is placed on top of the left hand on the solar plexus, to reinforce the flow of energy.*

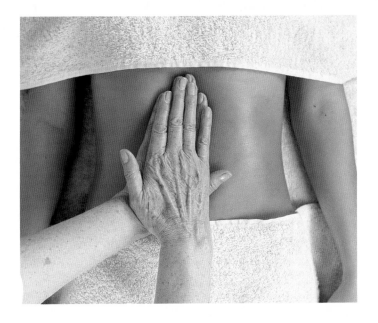

51 ▷ *Oil is applied to the feet and legs. Pressure is then applied to lymphatic points below the toes.*

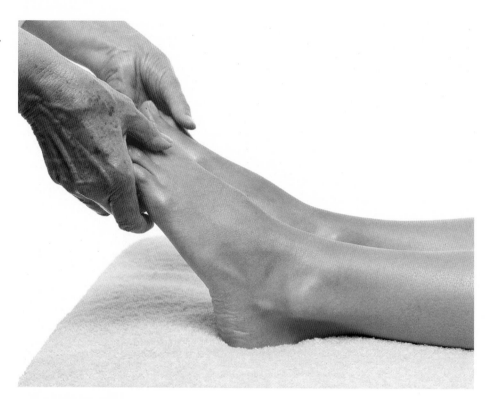

52 ▷ *A sliding movement, working from the toes to the ankles, helps drain lymph and release fluid retention.*

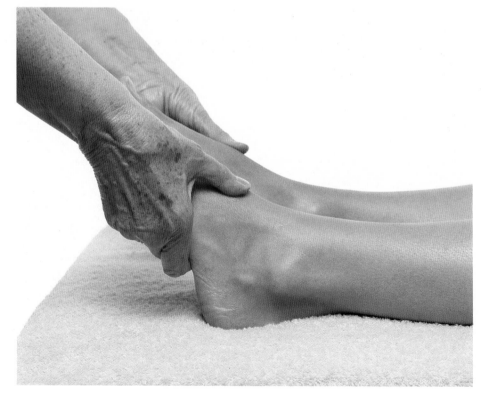

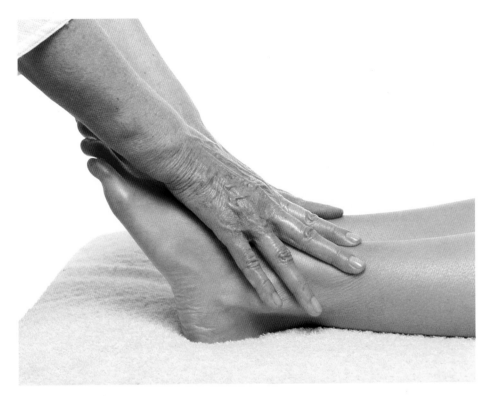

53 ◁ *Circular movements of the fingers around the ankles relieve fluid retention. From the ankles, the movement is continued by sliding the hands firmly up to the tops of the legs to help both circulation and lymph flow.*

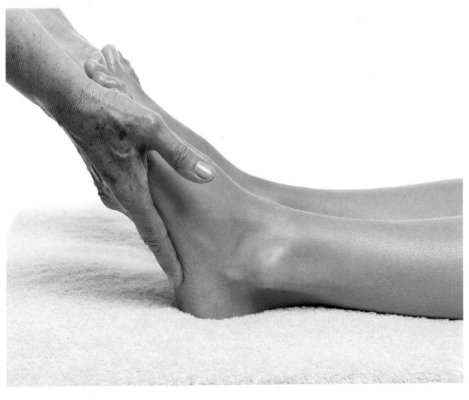

54 ◁ *The hands are placed flat on the soles of the feet. This is always done at the end of the treatment to rebalance the flow of energy.*

Aromatherapy treatment in pregnancy

Pregnancy can be one of the most exciting times of a woman's life – the mystery and miracle of creating another human life. It is also a time of great change, both physical and emotional, which can lead to a number of minor problems. It is important, however, to remember that having a baby is not an illness, no matter how many visits to medical practitioners may be involved. As a complement to today's advanced medical care, aromatherapy has an important role to play in helping a woman through her pregnancy. Over the years, I have devised a complete treatment for pregnancy, involving both a specific massage with specialized aromatic products for treatment both in the clinic and home care.

I always encourage women who wish to become pregnant to follow a programme of preconceptual care for both themselves and their partners. In my experience, a couple who are prepared for conception lay the foundations for a better pregnancy.

APPROACH TO PREGNANCY

There are numerous things a pregnant woman can do to help herself and her unborn child – such as eating well and avoiding alcohol, cigarettes and drugs of any kind. A pregnant mother's mental attitude to her pregnancy is very important. All the baby's organs are formed in the first few months, and whatever the mother feels, thinks and does will have an effect on it.

THE TREATMENT

The aromatherapy massage treatment for pregnant women is done in two stages. Stage one is for the client who is just pregnant, when she can still lie on her abdomen. The aromatherapy massage is the same as usual, but omitting all pressure points and using only tangerine body oil.

Stage two is for the client in the more advanced stages of pregnancy, when she is no longer able to lie on her abdomen. At this time, she sits up on the massage couch, sideways, with her feet resting on a stool, a pillow on her lap on which to rest her arms, and a towel around her chest and legs to keep them warm.

We first massage the neck and back with tangerine body oil, as these areas are the seat of much tension. Then the client lies on her back, propped up by pillows under her head and legs, or however she feels most comfortable, and is given a facial, using an oil chosen according to the quality of her skin.

Then we work on her breasts (avoiding the nipples), solar plexus, abdomen and legs, again using tangerine body oil.

The client may arrive feeling a little tired or nervous; the abdomen is often very tight and the baby tends to move around a lot. When the massage is over, it is amazing how often a client remarks on how the baby has settled down and how wonderfully relaxed her abdomen feels.

The client is always left to rest for 10 minutes or so after her massage, with a refreshing mask on her face. By the time she gets up, she feels strong and relaxed.

A weekly treatment is best, but this will obviously depend on the time available to the individual client. Fortnightly or even monthly treatments can still provide excellent care.

What does the treatment do?

- It is relaxing It helps to stop the build-up of tension, especially in the neck and shoulders and, in the later stages of pregnancy, in the lower back, which is sometimes affected by the extra weight of the baby.
- It is uplifting It improves the flow of energy and minimizes fatigue, which is quite usual during the first three months of pregnancy and again towards the end. The aroma of tangerine is also very refreshing.
- It is revitalizing It improves skin tone, helping to reduce small imperfections and spots.
- It improves the circulation Veins tend to become more apparent in pregnancy, and there is a greater tendency to varicose veins, thread veins and hemorrhoids. This is therefore particularly important.
- It stimulates lymphatic drainage and the elimination of toxic wastes from the system This is of great importance during pregnancy because of a greater tendency to fluid retention, which is often visible as a swelling in the ankles and legs.
- It tones muscles This combats the aches and pains that are sometimes caused by distended ligaments, and alleviates any tendency to cramp, which can occur towards the fifth month of pregnancy.
- It maintains the skin's suppleness and elasticity This helps prevent stretch marks, which often appear around the fifth month.
- It induces a general feeling of wellbeing The therapeutic effect of the essential oils coupled with the massage induces physical and mental relaxation.
- It prepares for childbirth Regular aromatherapy helps keep the whole system relaxed and in harmony, and so prepares it for childbirth.

THE ESSENTIAL OILS FOR PREGNANCY

It is important to be cautious in the use of essential oils when you are pregnant. It is not the case that because a product is natural it is necessarily good. Many essential oils are not suitable in pregnancy, because a baby could absorb too much from its mother. Any essential oil that stimulates menstruation is not suitable, particularly at the beginning of pregnancy.

The principle pregnancy oil that I use is tangerine. It has a pleasantly refreshing smell, has a very therapeutic harmonizing effect on both mind and body, and is excellent for preventing stretch marks.

Suitable oils

As a general guide, the following essential oils can all be used during pregnancy. Always use ½ to 1 per cent essential oil in a vegetable oil, such as jojoba, sesame or almond.

Cajuput, eucalyptus, niaouli, pine: all good for colds, bronchitis, influenza and sinusitis

Camomile: good for the digestive tract, calming and soothing to the skin

Geranium: always used in a low dosage of ½ per cent, good for blood circulation

Incense: has a general uplifting effect

Lavender: good in cases of general fatigue, tension, aches and pains and skin irritations

Lemon: good for high blood pressure and veins

Neroli: calming for the nervous system, soothing for the skin

Orange: fortifying and a tonic for the nervous system

Sandalwood: good for the urinary tract and for general control of fluid retention in the body as, for example, when legs and ankles are swelling

Tangerine: the best pregnancy oil of all, with a general harmonizing effect on the mind and body, and good for preventing stretch marks

GENERAL ADVICE

There are several things I advise expectant mothers to do to make pregnancy easier and to contribute to the good health of her baby.

Diet

Diet is important. The future mother has a responsibility to her baby to eat well during her pregnancy, as the baby will benefit greatly from healthy and natural foods. It is wise to eat plenty of vegetables, either raw or cooked, and to have a good intake of protein. Fresh foods are generally preferable to processed ones, both because processing reduces their nutritional value and because of the additives so many of them contain.

Morning sickness can be very trying, though it does not usually last very long. There are several simple measures which can help considerably, such as eating little and often, taking solids rather than liquids, avoiding rich, heavy or fried foods, eating slowly and chewing well. Breakfast in bed can help a lot. Camomile tea is calming and has a soothing effect on the stomach.

Rest

It is important to take plenty of rest during pregnancy. I recommend at least an hour's total rest each day, feet up, and doing nothing more taxing than listening to music or reading.

Exercise

This is good within reason, particularly if you were used to taking exercise before you became pregnant. Swimming is excellent, as is yoga. Taking a regular gentle walk in the evening is a good idea, as it speeds up the circulation and encourages sleep. Strenuous exercise, however, is not advised, and skiing and horseriding, in particular, should be avoided as they carry the danger of heavy falls.

Work

I believe that it is wise to stop work at least six weeks before the confinement. Unfortunately, however, this is not always possible, but taking as much rest as possible when out of the workplace is advisable.

PROBLEMS DURING PREGNANCY

There are a number of problems that can beset a woman in pregnancy; most of them are quite minor but they can be distressing. Aromatherapy massage can help these, as can the use of tangerine body oil and lavender bath oil.

- Varicose veins can occur, due to the abnormal dilation of veins caused by hormonal change. It is advisable to rest with your legs elevated, not to wear tight boots or constricting undergarments, and to avoid excessive heat, such as that caused by hot baths, sunbathing, and hot depilatory wax. Support tights can help, and walking regularly encourages a healthy circulation. Treatment may include compresses of cold water with Dermarome aromatic lotion on the feet and legs. Imported from Switzerland, this is a blend of essential oils in a special base that makes it possible to dilute in water. Home massage can be done once a day on the legs, working with an upward movement towards the heart and using essential oil of geranium in low dosage in soya vegetable oil.

- Stretch marks are caused by the destruction of the elastic fibres of the skin. They tend to appear around the fifth month of pregnancy, when the abdomen is starting to enlarge and to stretch the skin. Daily massage on the breasts, abdomen and buttocks with tangerine essence in jojoba oil is excellent, and should be done by the expectant mother at home, morning and night, for the whole of her pregnancy. In fact, it is a good idea to continue massage for a few weeks after the birth to help muscle tissue return to its normal state.

- The breasts must be well cared for throughout pregnancy. Wear a good supporting cotton bra and massage morning and night with some tangerine body oil, being careful not to touch the nipples.

✗ A faint feeling is sometimes brought on by standing up too quickly. This is caused by the enlarged uterus pressing on the lower vena cava, which is the large blood vessel bringing blood back to the head from the lower part of the body. Try sleeping with two pillows, taking a rest after eating, drinking camomile tea, and massaging the solar plexus with camomile body oil.

✗ Backache is common in pregnancy because of the extra weight of the baby. Rest is a must, and massaging with oils of lavender and sandalwood in either soya or sesame vegetable oil is helpful in relaxing tense muscles.

A calming bath with lavender bath oil also helps to relax overstretched muscles. The bathwater must be neither too hot, which is tiring and bad for the veins and blood pressure, nor too cold, which could cause the uterus to contract; the best temperature is one of 37°C (98°F). If you are using pure essence, use three drops well mixed with the bathwater. And do not stay in the bath for too long – 10 minutes is long enough and more can be tiring.

✗ Disturbed sleep patterns are common in pregnancy. Relaxing herb teas such as lemon balm and relaxing baths with lavender or camomile, followed by an application of neroli body oil, are all helpful.

✗ Fluid retention can cause swollen legs and ankles, particularly in hot weather and if you have to stand for long periods of time. We recommend putting the feet up and using compresses of cold water and Dermarome aromatic lotion on the feet and legs. A body oil made up of lavender and sandalwood in soya, sesame or wheatgerm vegetable oil should also help. If the condition worsens, consult your doctor.

✗ Constipation is another of those irritating problems that can occur during pregnancy. The best way to deal with this is to eat plenty of fresh raw or cooked fruit and vegetables, and to drink a cup of hot boiled water first thing in the morning, with or without lemon juice. Back massage is also helpful.

✗ Itching can be caused by too much acidity in the body, and it is a good idea to drink plenty of mineral water and to avoid too much sugar. Lavender baths are excellent for the skin, as is a body oil of sandalwood and lavender in jojoba vegetable oil.

✗ Scars may become redder and more noticeable. Massaging the area with camomile and lavender in wheatgerm vegetable oil will help.

✗ The skin can change during pregnancy. Some people will have the best complexion they have ever had, others will experience very dry or very oily skin for the first time in their lives. It is most important to assess the situation and to counteract it, which is one reason why it is advisable to contact an aromatherapist who can analyse your skin condition at each stage of pregnancy. Aromatherapy treatment is excellent in that it involves the care of both face and body together.

One problem that often occurs around the fourth or fifth month of pregnancy is a skin pigmentation known as chloasma, which causes brown patches to develop on the face. These are due to hormonal changes and usually disappear after the birth. Exposure to the sun makes the brown marks worse, so stay in the shade or use a good sun block.

The nails may become weak and brittle during pregnancy. Massage them, especially around the cuticles, morning and night, with a mixture of essential oil of lemon in almond oil.

Post-natal Depression

The great majority of women do not suffer any kind of adverse reaction after birth, except to be emotional, easily upset, and overtired. For a minority of them, however, it can be a very different story, with a change of mood some time after the initial excitement following the birth. This usually coincides with the sudden change in hormone level brought on by the start of lactation.

A new mother can be very sensitive, prone to weeping and, at times, liable to become irrational and depressed. Loss of sleep and excessive fatigue lead to anxiety, panic attacks and disproportionate worry. This is now recognized as a post-natal depressive illness, which can vary from a mild state to very severe cases that are, thankfully, rare.

Fortunately, all degrees of post-natal depression can be treated, and full recovery follows. Aromatherapy is known to be helpful in preventing cases of post-natal depression; the use of essential oils certainly seems to make life a lot more pleasant and to help counteract any tendency towards negative feelings of this kind.

The Role of the Aromatherapist

The numerous pregnancy treatments that I and my therapists have given over the past 20 years have proved to be very successful. It is exciting – and gratifying – for us to see so many grateful mothers, especially when they bring their healthy new babies to show us. We call them our aromatherapy babies.

The support of a positive and sympathetic aromatherapist can be of tremendous value to a pregnant woman. The part played by the personality of the aromatherapist is very important – a good listener encourages the expectant mother to ask about any problems and anxieties she may have. Common sense and humour can work wonders to alleviate worries, be they real or imaginary. However, the therapist also needs a sound knowledge of what can happen to a woman in pregnancy so that she will be aware of any problem necessitating medical attention.

ONE WOMAN'S EXPERIENCE . . .

Madeleine Bell had been a keen advocate of aromatherapy for some years and it seemed only natural to her to continue her treatments when she became pregnant. She found the aromatherapy massage to be of even greater benefit than before, and sessions spent with her therapist to be a particular comfort at a time when she felt more vulnerable and in greater need of reassurance than usual.

The prospect of having her first baby at the age of 39 obviously gave her some cause for concern, but her regular treatments calmed her and helped her to look forward to the birth with confidence. She felt strong, both physically and emotionally, throughout her pregnancy. She had virtually no morning sickness and no backache, nor really any other discomfort. She can't, of course, be sure exactly how much of this was due to aromatherapy, but feels certain that it helped her a great deal.

After the birth of her baby, Madeleine recovered very quickly – no doubt thanks, at least in part, to continued aromatherapy treatments. She now has a lovely little girl, Sabrina, who is both healthy and happy. Madeleine soon started to give her aromatherapy massage as part of her daily routine. She clearly enjoys it – she is, after all, an aromatherapy baby!

Massage in pregnancy

These are the main massage movements for the more advanced stage of pregnancy, when the client is no longer able to lie on her abdomen. The principal essential oil I use in pregnancy is tangerine.

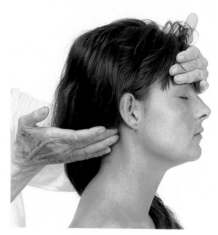

1 △ *Pressure against the cranium bone releases tension. The sliding movement liberates magnetic flow.*

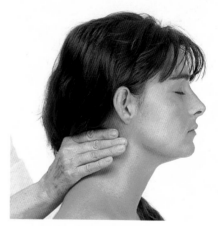

2 △ *The neck is gently massaged to release tension.*

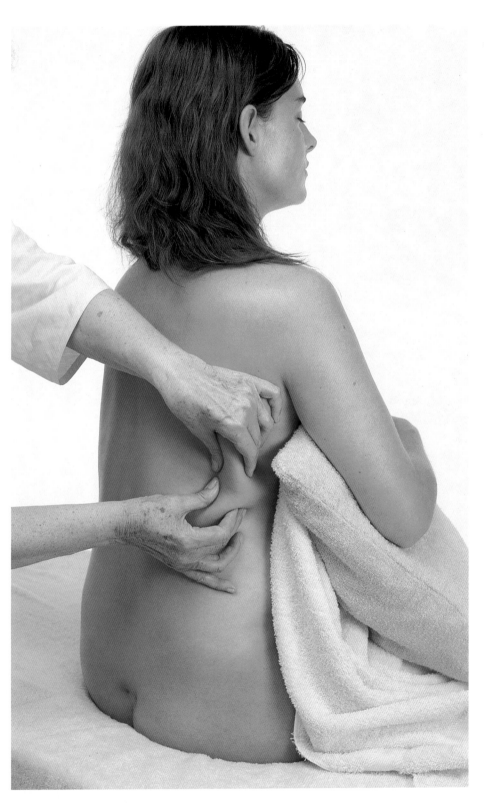

3 ◁ *Having
applied the oil to
the body with a
movement of*
effleurage, *a*
petrissage
*movement is used,
sliding and
kneading from
buttocks to
shoulders, which
releases waste
materials and
improves muscle
tonicity.*

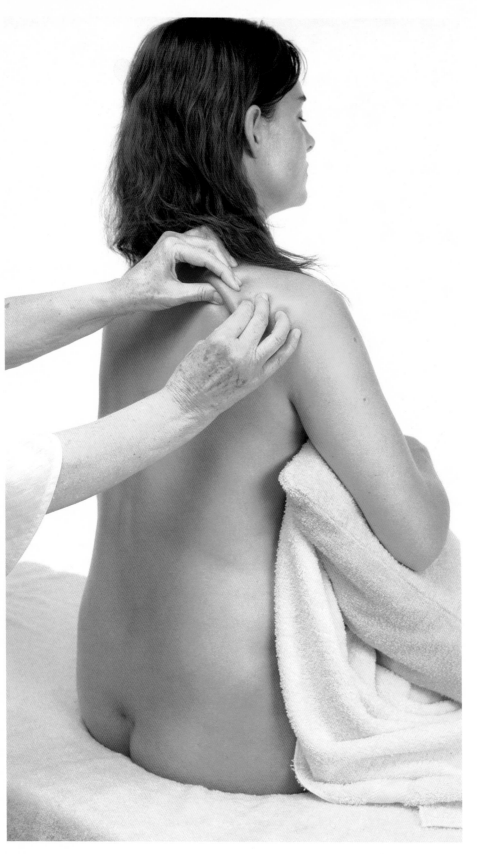

4 ◁ *The tissues are rolled up with the thumbs from buttocks to shoulders in order to help eliminate waste materials and to encourage lymphatic flow.*

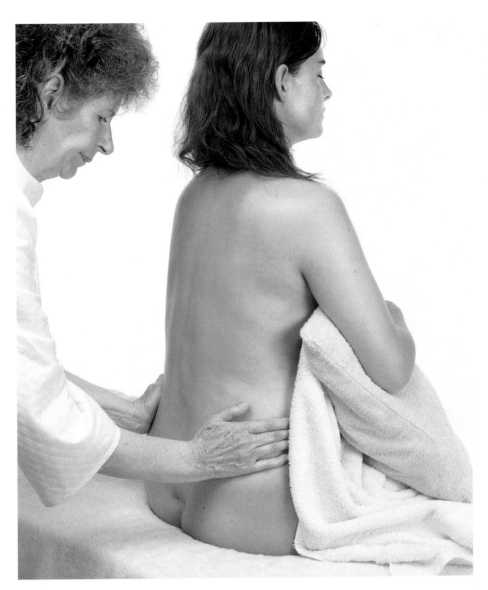

5 ◁ *A fanning movement on the lumbar area relieves congestion and strengthens the back muscles.*

6 △ Petrissage *on the back of the neck helps to relieve tension.*

7 △ *A sliding movement on the lymph points encourages lymphatic drainage.*

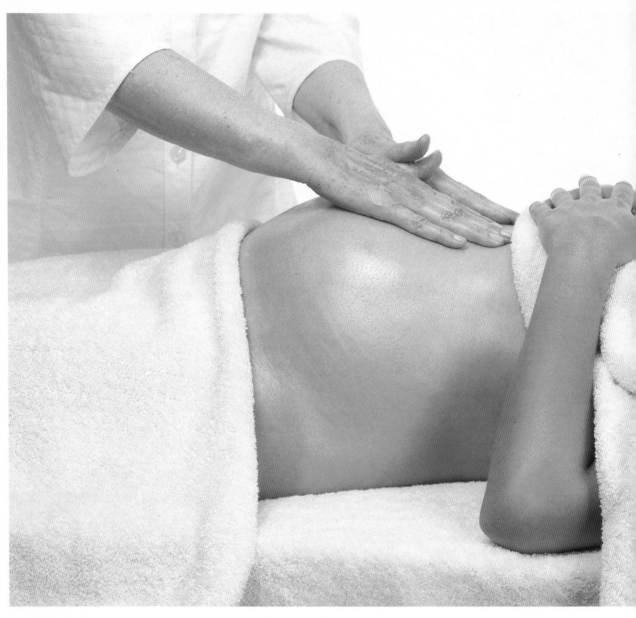

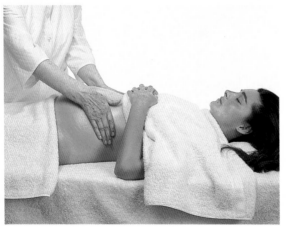
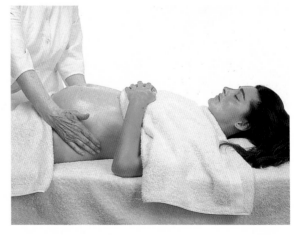

8 ◁ *Oil is applied all over the abdominal area to feed the tissues and to help prevent stretch marks.*

11 ▽ *The solar plexus is massaged in an anti-clockwise direction to release stress.*

9 ◁ ◁ *A gentle massage movement covers the whole of the abdomen, which helps to relax it.*

10 ◁ *As the movement is repeated many times, there is a calming and soothing influence on the baby.*

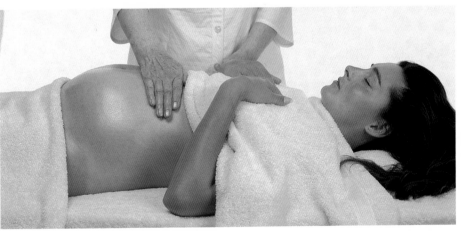

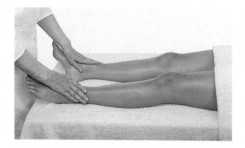

12 ◁ ◁ *Oil is applied to both legs with a movement of effleurage.*

13 ◁ *The hands then slide up to the knees using an effleurage movement.*

14 ◁ *Both hands slide further up the leg to the top of the thighs using an effleurage movement. This is a soothing action, which also helps to spread the oil.*

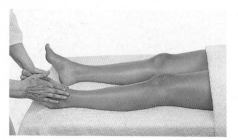

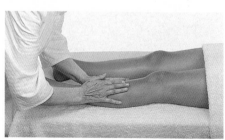

15 ◁ ◁ *Working on one leg at a time, circular movements help to liberate fluid.*

16 ◁ *The hands slide up to the knee, and a circular movement around the knee helps the lymphatic flow and eliminates waste materials.*

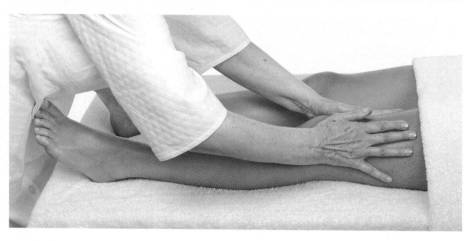

17 ◁ *Hands work on the thighs to improve both blood circulation and lymphatic drainage.*

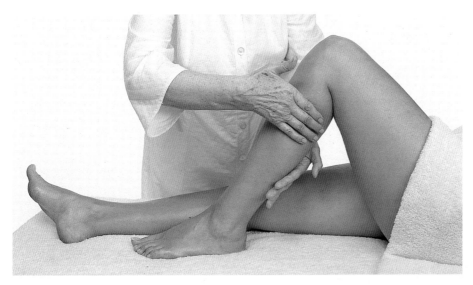

18 ◁ *The calf muscle is lifted and supported with one hand, while being massaged with the other.*

19 ◁ *Work is done on the back of the thigh up to the top of the leg, in order to liberate lymph.*

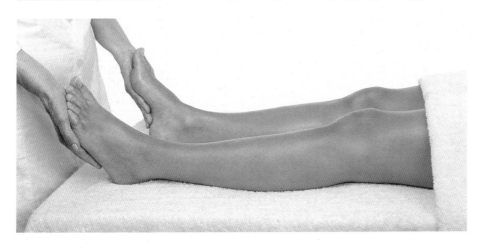

20 ◁ *To finish, the hands are placed on the soles of the feet to rebalance the energy field.*

Treating different conditions

Aromatherapy can be used to treat a range of different conditions and problems, which may be both physical and psychological. Here we look at its versatility and scope.

Stress

The word 'stress' is used incessantly. It has become part of our everyday language. But what does it really mean?

To be suffering from stress means being in a state of high tension which, if not controlled, can eventually be the precursor of a more serious physical or mental illness.

Stress is more often known under the name of nervous tension. What we mean when we talk about a stressful situation is one which is putting so much pressure on us that we are not able to cope with it. This state of stress is becoming so common that the medical profession has now acknowledged its seriousness by convening many symposia and congresses on the subject.

It is now recognized as a serious threat to our health. It is a potential killer, and we must pay great attention to mastering it before it masters us.

How The Body Reacts

Stress leads to chronic fatigue, depression and the need for pep pills, alcohol and drugs. The noisy, violent and bustling modern world engenders much stress and the highly sensitive individual can be greatly affected.

Women tend, on the whole, to resist stress better. They are more flexible and are used to dealing with so many conflicting situations that they have often become adept at adapting quickly to the changing demands of the moment.

Differences in temperament are important in relation to the response to stress. Presented with a piece of bad news, for example, one person may react by shouting, crying or getting angry. By a quick externalization of his or her feelings in this way, the subject may become prone to high blood pressure, cardiovascular difficulties, obesity and so on.

Another type of person remains calm and controlled, with a stiff upper lip, showing no external signs of anger or grief. By keeping everything in, this person is more prone to infectious diseases, rheumatism, even cancer, and his or her resistance to infection is diminished by the perpetual assault on the nervous system, eating away the energies.

People who fall between these extremes take bad news in their stride. They do not panic, they collect themselves, and then let things ride for a while. These are the lucky people, who know the secret of resisting stress.

Assessing The Problem

Stress is our daily companion. Its effect is cumulative and becomes harmful when we cannot cope.

So how do we assess stress? If it affects us only occasionally, harmony can be brought back relatively easily by certain measures adapted to the requirement. If it affects us repeatedly, on the other hand, we are likely to suffer a variety of symptoms. These include insomnia or poor, agitated sleep and fatigue; palpitations and irregular heart beat; aches and pains; lack of interest and motivation, and even personal neglect; fits of uncontrollable crying; irritability and unexpressed anger; nausea or food craving; fear of the future; loss of memory and inability to concentrate. Other problems which are now recognized as being caused by stress include certain skin conditions, such as eczema, herpes and psoriasis, and – more seriously – cancer and degenerative diseases.

Stress diminishes the quality of the immune system and opens the door to many ills. We must learn self-discipline and the ability to resist the many attacks against us. It is not so much what happens to us that is important as the way in which we react to it. We cannot change the world, but we can change our attitude to it.

How Aromatherapy Can Help

Aromatherapy acts on the nervous system, which is our most subtle system and the one that is most easily disturbed in the modern world.

When a client is suffering from stress, we work on a programme to help her to relax and to bring her back to a more harmonious way of life. In this way, we hope that she will learn how to cope with these specific forms of stress that assail her in her life. Weekly treatments are very beneficial and help to check the build-up of tensions.

The consultation

The first thing we do during the consultation is to assess, with the client, what her main stresses are. Good common sense is a useful ally in consultation. We rarely tell the client anything that she does not already know, but the fact that we are able to analyse the situation together often clarifies her mind and helps her to find a solution.

For example, we saw a young doctor who was finding it difficult to cope with the dual demands of her profession and her young baby. On analysis, the conflict was settled by a simple compromise: part-time work, part-time nanny. So many women live with this perpetual conflict of family or work.

The fact that we are able to discuss her problems with a client automatically releases much of her stress. Sometimes she even manages to see the funny side of the situation. It is important for people not to take themselves too seriously: a good laugh is an excellent medicine.

Massage

Aromatherapy massage works primarily on the autonomic nervous system, which is part of the nervous system over which we have no control, such as the beating of the heart. This means that it automatically relaxes the client.

We work on pressure points on either side of the spine which function like a series of little power stations to produce energy. In this way, we induce a state of release of tension and stimulate the entire organism to work better.

It is amazing how hard, congested tissues and muscles give way under the fingers. When we look at a client's face after her massage, her newly relaxed appearance often seems to have taken years off her. The soothing movements we use on the face and head have a pleasantly hypnotic quality, while working on the solar plexus in an anti-clockwise direction relaxes the nerve centres and helps to release inner stresses.

The massage of the entire body gives her a feeling of wholeness and well-being, which often plunges her deep into a beneficial sleep. It has a reharmonizing effect, working on the electromagnetic field to rebalance her energy level. Many painful areas are the result of energy blockages and of a build-up of toxins, which are relieved by skilful massage techniques.

Essential oils

The essential oils we use during the massage of the face and body have a double action. Firstly, they work by scent, and secondly, they are absorbed through the skin into the bloodstream. They are powerful allies in the fight against stress.

We choose essential oils for their calming and rebalancing properties. There is a wide variety of these at our disposal – for example, bergamot, camomile, lavender, marjoram, neroli, orange, petitgrain and vetivert.

These are used either in a single essential oil preparation with a vegetable oil, such as jojoba, soya bean, sesame, St John's wort or wheatgerm, or in a combination of two or three essential oils, again with a vegetable oil.

Then, at the end of the treatment, a rejuvenating mask is placed on the client's face, and eye pads, soaked in rose water, orange blossom water or camomile lotion, are placed on her eyes. She is then left for 10 minutes to relax and, if she is so inclined, to sleep.

HOME TREATMENT

We explain to our client that she can carry on the work done in our consulting rooms by treating herself at home, using much the same essential oils as those used in the clinic. We do not like to recommend too many products, so as not to add still more pressure to someone who is already overloaded.

The most popular recommendation is a bath oil. We recommend clients to have three or four aromatic baths a week, using a calming and relaxing formulation. If there is no time for a bath or the client prefers a shower, a foot-bath can be useful, or she can just sponge her body with a wet sponge to which one drop only of essential oil has been applied.

In addition, a single drop of the essential oil of vetivert – which we call the essential oil of tranquillity – will bring a great release of tension when applied anti-clockwise to the solar plexus. We recommend repeating this morning and night.

We also recommend what we call a weekly therapeutic evening, when a light meal is eaten and an aromatic bath taken, followed by early bed – perhaps listening to some music or reading. The beauty of this evening is that the client is not under any obligations, so that she has a chance to recharge her batteries.

What You Can Do

Life is so busy for many people that there seems to be hardly any time left for themselves. We emphasize to clients that too long a period of stress can lead to disaster. A short holiday and a change of scenery helps them to break the routine and to regain a fresh and balanced view of their lives.

Diet

A good diet has proved to be a great help in reducing stress and there are some foods that are best avoided during stressful periods. We advise our clients to avoid red meat, white flour and products made with it, sugar (honey is better), processed foods and to limit the amount of fat they eat. We recommend simple, wholesome food. We advocate the food combining diet, which means not eating carbohydrates and protein at the same meal, as the digestion of these two elements is quite different and their combination overloads the system and thus causes poor digestion.

We recommend drinking very little – if at all – with meals, so as not to disturb the digestive process in the stomach. In particular, it is better to avoid coffee, white wine and spirits, especially in the evening.

Just as important as what we eat is how we eat. It is good to eat slowly and to chew each mouthful well. It is also important to eat in peace and harmony. Arguing during meals is definitely not recommended, as it turns even the best food into poison. When there is no time to eat at leisure, it is better to eat yoghurt or a piece of fruit, or even to have just a quick drink, than to swallow a sandwich at full speed, as this upsets the digestive and nervous systems of the body.

Meditation

Meditation has been shown to have a relaxing and beneficial effect on people, and is now becoming very popular. It works on the principle that it is only by getting in touch with their inner selves that people are able to develop sufficient inner strength that acts as a filter against all stressful situations.

Even 15 minutes' meditation a day is better than nothing. If, however, you are not inclined to meditate, just close your eyes, think about the day before you and gather in your energies towards a more balanced day.

Tips for relaxation

Everyone has their own preference as to how they unwind. The important thing is to make sure that you really do get enough rest and relaxation.

Exercise is very helpful in the reduction of stress. Yoga is particularly good, as is walking in parks or, better still, in the country.

One excellent exercise, which may sound odd but actually rebalances energy levels, is to lie spreadeagled on your stomach, preferably on the lawn, so that the solar plexus is in contact with the earth and discharges any excess of positive electricity or the wrong type of magnetism. It can also be done on a bed or floor and is still beneficial, but this is obviously not as effective.

Whenever you feel angry, wash your hands ten times under a running tap. This takes away the wrong type of magnetism from the body through the hands. Never go to bed angry at night, as this state of mind works on the subconscious level and has negative repercussions on your whole being.

Deep abdominal breathing has a calming and reharmonizing effect on the system, particularly if you are feeling nervous, anxious or fearful. Simply inhale through the nose – the rib cage should expand forwards and sideways – and exhale through the mouth, breathing slowly, gently, evenly and rhythmically.

Music is a wonderful therapy, whether you are playing, singing or simply listening to it. Painting is a useful expression of your innermost feelings.

A fragrancer is effective in a bedroom to release a calming aroma for a couple of hours before retiring. Try a relaxing essential oil, such as bergamot, camomile, lavender or neroli, depending on taste and preference.

A herb tea before retiring induces a better sleep. Try lime blossom, lemon verbena, camomile, melissa, skullcap or marjoram.

Good organization saves a lot of irritation and frustration. An excellent axiom to follow is that if you live for the day, the morrow will take care of itself. To accept what cannot be changed would, for many people, be half the battle.

ONE WOMAN'S EXPERIENCE...

Cara Minton has run a highly pressurized business for the last ten years and, as a result, her lifestyle has been fast and furious. Then a year ago, things became too much for her.

She felt that her nerves were on edge and she suddenly realized that there was more to life than working flat out for 10 hours a day, five days a week. A friend suggested that she try aromatherapy.

Almost as soon as she embarked on aromatherapy, she felt that her problems had begun to disappear. She found it a wonderful tonic, both for the relaxing massage and for the sage advice she received as her therapist talked through her problems with her and helped her cope with them.

Cara is now much more relaxed. The tension has entirely gone from her shoulders and, perhaps most significant of all, she works only three days a week. She is truly grateful for the change aromatherapy has made to her life.

Skin Care

The skin is the largest organ of the body and it performs many important tasks. It plays a vital role as an external and internal secretion gland. It has different layers and appendages – such as sweat and sebaceous glands, hair and nails. Internally, it produces hormones and enzymes. It is both strong and elastic, and protects all the internal organs from external attack. And it cushions them from both external shock and chemical aggression, thanks to its layer of fat.

The skin prevents the evaporation of water, thus controlling changes in temperature. It produces heat, electricity and radiation. Like the other tissues of the body, it breathes, absorbing oxygen and expelling carbon dioxide.

It provides protection against germs and viruses. It also rejects impurities and toxins from the body, and has been recognized in this capacity as a 'second kidney'.

How Essential Oils Affect the Skin

Essential oils are absorbed through the skin and penetrate its deepest layers. The main property of all essential oils is that they are highly antiseptic, though at different degrees, depending on the essence chosen. They help speed up the removal of old skin cells and thus encourage the production of new cells.

Essential oils help muscles to regain a healthy condition and aid the soft tissue to get rid of excess fluid and waste materials or, if required, to restore lost hydration. They also act as blood regulators, improving the blood circulation. With the help of pressure points on nerve centres, the essential oils help to regulate the nervous system, making it more alert to impulses and quicker to react.

In our clinic, we use body and face oils which are made up of essential oils mixed with vegetable oils. The percentage for the face varies between 1 and

3 per cent essential oil to vegetable oil, depending on the condition being treated and the strength of essential oil being used. For the body, it varies between 2 and 5 per cent essential oil to vegetable oil.

FACE PRODUCTS

Deep cleansing is essential, especially if you use make-up. Apply the cleansing milk or oil to face and neck, using gentle circular movements. Remove with tissue and repeat until the tissue comes away clean. Next, apply herbal lotion with cotton wool to tone the skin. Evian spray, which has an excellent alkaline action and counteracts any acidity in the skin, is good for all skin types.

A nourishing and moisturizing face oil or cream should then be applied to a clean skin morning and night. Apply it all over the face and neck and around the eyes, with gentle stroking movements. If you use make-up, do not apply it until at least 15 minutes later, to make sure there is no excess oil left and that it has all been absorbed. If there is still some excess oil after this time, blot it with a tissue, then apply make-up.

Depending on the quality of the skin, deep cleansing should be done with a face shampoo, either four times a week for oily skins, or once a week for dry, sensitive skins. Face shampoo is a useful product. It should be applied gently to the skin with a little lukewarm water, massaging it in with circular movements of the fingertips over those areas that need particularly deep cleansing, which are usually the nose and chin areas. Rinse off, then tone.

A face mask is a must, either once or twice a week, depending on skin type. This can be either a deep cleansing, highly antiseptic mask for oily skins; a lighter mask for normal skins; a soothing mask for sensitive skins; or a rejuvenating mask for mature skins. Apply a small amount evenly over face and neck, avoiding the eye area. Leave for 5 to 10 minutes, then rinse off gently with lukewarm water, being careful not to drag the skin. Pat dry and then apply face oil or cream.

NORMAL SKIN

A healthy, normal skin is neither too dry nor too oily, and is smooth and even in tone.

Cleansing We usually recommend a face shampoo, to be used in the morning two or three times a week. At other times, it is best to use a cleansing milk containing rose or camomile. This should be followed either by a lotion of rose water or orange blossom water, or by Evian spray.

Face oil Face oil should be applied to a clean skin, morning and evening. Make-up can be applied 15 minutes later. For young skins, we recommend 2 per cent essential oils of either basil, camomile, sandalwood or ylang ylang in sesame vegetable oil. For mature skins, we recommend a face oil containing 3 per cent essential oil, choosing from rose, patchouli, sage or geranium, in jojoba or wheatgerm vegetable oil.

Face mask We also suggest the application, twice weekly, of a refreshing and slightly cleansing herbal mask. This should be alternated with the application of pulp of apricots, which you can prepare by liquidizing fresh apricots in a blender. Leave on the skin for 10 minutes and rinse off with rose water.

DRY, SENSITIVE SKIN

This sort of skin is very fine, with a tendency to line quickly. It can also be highly sensitive, and is sometimes congested with thread veins. It is important to protect and revitalize this type of skin in order to prevent the appearance of further broken capillaries.

Cleansing We recommend a cleansing milk containing rose, raspberry or cucumber, followed by a camomile lotion made up as follows: pour 150 ml (¼ pint) of boiling water on to two medium flowers of Roman camomile and allow to infuse for 20 minutes. Then strain the mixture into a bottle and keep in a cool, dark place. A fresh supply should be prepared every 5 to 7 days. Other lotions that can be used include orange blossom water; witch-hazel, which is very decongestive; rose water; cucumber juice, made by putting a cucumber in a juice extractor; and Evian spray.

Face oil For young skins, we recommend 2 per cent essential oil of either camomile, sandalwood, geranium or neroli in wheatgerm vegetable oil. For more mature skins, we recommend 2 per cent essential oil of either rose, patchouli, sandalwood, cypress or geranium in wheatgerm or jojoba vegetable oil.

Face mask A gentle, soothing herbal mask should be used once a week. Alternatively, you can use compresses with the lotions already detailed. Cut a piece of gauze roughly to the size of your face and soak it in the lotion. Squeeze out any excess, place on the face and leave for 10 minutes.

COMBINATION SKIN

This consists of localized areas of either too dry or too oily skin. It requires a treatment that will help all the conditions concerned.

Cleansing We recommend a face shampoo twice a week and a cleansing milk made with either cucumber or rose. Follow with rose water, orange blossom water, Evian spray, or home-made camomile lotion (see above).

Face oil By mixing different essential oils, we are able to make up a product that is suitable for the whole face. We recommend 3 per cent essential oils of sandalwood, which is soothing and hydrating; patchouli, which is nourishing and revitalizing; and geranium, which rebalances blood circulation; in jojoba vegetable oil, which is unusual in being good for both dry and oily skins.

Face mask To counteract the excessive oiliness of the central panel, we recommend applying a weekly camphor mask, which is highly antiseptic, refreshing and refines the skin texture of the whole face.

In addition, apply a mask just once a week to the oily panel. This should be made up of clay powder mixed with water, to which you then add one drop only of essential oil of bay, bergamot or lemon. Clay has invaluable properties and, combined with essential oils, ensures that the central panel gradually becomes less oily and that the face gets a more uniform appearance.

General advice We often find that clients with excessive oiliness, even when it is only on the central panel, are not following a healthy diet. We suggest they check that they are not eating over-rich food or drinking too much alcohol or sweet drinks. Some make-up can be too heavy and clog the skin, so always be sure to use a light make-up instead.

OILY SKIN

Oily skin has a shiny appearance, is often quite sallow, and tends to be coarse to the touch, with a lot of impurities and a tendency to blackheads. It looks generally devitalized, and needs deep cleansing and exfoliation to help with the regeneration of cells and the refinement of texture.

Cleansing Cleansing is very important, particularly if you use make-up – this type of skin tends to absorb more make-up. A face shampoo should be used every day and, to remove make-up, use a camphor cleansing milk or one specifically for oily skin.

Then use a lotion made with lavender, peppermint or thyme. Make this at home by pouring 150 ml (¼ pint) of boiling water on to ¼ teaspoon of the dried herb. Allow to infuse for 15 minutes, then strain into a bottle and keep in a cool, dark place. Prepare a fresh supply every 5 to 7 days. Alternatively, make a lotion with tomato or grapefruit put through a juice extractor – this will complete the cleansing and ensure that the skin is quite free of any impurities. Evian spray is particularly good.

I have always been against astringents, most of which contain alcohol and not only over-dehydrate the skin but actually stimulate the sebaceous glands to produce more sebum.

Face oil Many people believe that it is inappropriate to use an oily product on an oily skin. But essential oils are different. They help to rebalance the condition.

We recommend a face oil made up with very antiseptic essential oils that counteract the unbalanced skin. A formulation of 3 per cent essential oil of either bay, bergamot, juniper, lavender or lemon in sesame or soya vegetable oil is just right. If the skin is very dehydrated, jojoba vegetable oil is the best base.

Face mask This kind of skin produces a lot of impurities and must be well cleansed at all times. The importance of using a face mask is therefore obvious. A mask made with clay powder mixed with cucumber or carrot juice and one drop only of essential oil of bay, juniper or lemon can be used once a week, and should be alternated with a weekly camphor mask.

General advice Check your diet to make sure it is healthy. A vegetarian diet is helpful, at least for a while and especially during treatment. This, together with plenty of mineral water, helps eliminate toxic elements. Cleansing and purifying herb teas, such as thyme and wild pansy, are also particularly useful.

ACNE VULGARIS

This condition is more common at puberty, but may plague people for longer periods or at any time during their lives. Acneic skin is generally quite greasy, and usually slightly coarse, with enlarged ostii (the openings of the sebaceous glands on the surface of the skin), blackheads and infected spots, which can range from small to very large cystic conditions.

Cleansing Deep cleansing with face shampoo is essential, and should be done every day. Make sure that the face is well rinsed and patted dry with a tissue, as towels can help to spread the infection. Camphor cleansing milk is also good, even if clients do not use make-up. In fact, we usually suggest that they refrain from using make-up for a while, until the skin is in better condition. If it is necessary to use make-up, apply face oil 15 minutes beforehand to avoid spreading infection.

A good home-made lotion can be made using herbs of lavender, peppermint, rosemary and thyme (see page 108). Alternatively, you can try using Evian spray, or use freshly squeezed orange juice mixed with one-third rose water.

Face oil A face oil is important to keep the skin protected against further infection. Choose from bay, juniper, lavender, lemon, myrrh, niaouli or styrax, and use 3 per cent essential oil in soya vegetable oil.

Face mask Mix clay powder with water and one drop only of essential oil of either bay, lavender or lemon. Twice a week, we suggest using a camphor mask, or clay powder mixed with natural yoghurt. You can treat individual spots by applying just one drop of essential oil of niaouli on the spot head, which will dry it out and fight infection, but never use pure niaouli essence all over the face.

General advice Do not touch the spots and do not try to squeeze blackheads, as infections will usually follow. Again, a strict cleansing diet is recommended.

ACNE ROSACEA

This condition requires a different treatment from *Acne vulgaris*, as the skin can be sensitive and strong products are therefore not advisable. This condition usually happens later on in life, though it has been known to occur in women as young as 25. The main problem is a congestive state with, at the same time, the secondary one of large spots. The skin tends to be fine, and is usually dehydrated and quite acid.

Cleansing Cleansing milk with rose has a very decongestive effect. Tone with rose water, Evian spray, witch-hazel, camomile lotion or orange blossom water. Compresses of camomile lotion can be very soothing and help the tissues to look less inflamed.

Face oil We recommend 2 per cent essential oil of either Roman camomile, cypress, geranium, juniper, neroli, rose, sage or sandalwood in jojoba vegetable oil, which nourishes the skin without overfeeding it.

Face mask Masks should be light, decongestive and soothing. We recommend any made with azulene (extract of camomile), a herbal gel or plain yoghurt. Clay powder mixed with water can be applied on spots that do not come to a head; if they are infected alternate with one drop only of essential oil of niaouli, applied directly on top of the spot with a cottonbud.

General advice This condition is often linked to the menopause. In this case, the client must take particular care of her general state of health.

ALLERGIC SKIN

Allergic skin is usually very fine and hypersensitive. It reacts quickly to the touch and can show reactions, such as rashes, redness, dermatitis and sometimes eczema. This type of skin requires a lot of understanding and care.

Cleansing This must be gentle and soothing. We suggest rose cleansing milk, followed by camomile lotion and Evian spray, which is most useful for decongesting the skin. We recommend removing excess cleansing milk with damp cotton wool and then drying by gently applying a tissue to absorb excess moisture, while being careful not to rub. Compresses of camomile lotion and witch-hazel are very soothing.

Face oil Essential oils are excellent for allergic skins and rarely cause allergic reactions. The golden rule is to be cautious.

We have had clients who could not use cosmetic or perfumed products. Our method with this type of client is to use one essential oil at a time, mixed with jojoba vegetable oil. We might, for example, make up a 30 cc bottle of face oil, with just one drop of essential oil of Roman camomile, and then ask the client to use this. If everything goes well and she has no allergic reaction, we then try a second essence, using sandalwood, for example. Again, if she has no reaction, we follow the same method using neroli. When we are quite sure that she has had no reaction, we make up a face oil using all three essential oils at 1 per cent in jojoba oil.

Eczema

Pre-eczematic skin is excessively dry, in which case the treatment recommended for dry skin would be suitable (see page 107). When there are patches of eczema, we use only the mildest of products. If the eczema has reached the level of lesions, we refer the client to a doctor.

Cleansing We recommend a mild cleansing milk. Anything containing azulene (extract of camomile) is very beneficial. Compresses of camomile lotion are very soothing.

Face oil We recommend 1 per cent essential oil of either camomile, neroli or sandalwood in jojoba or wheatgerm vegetable oil. For weeping eczema we recommend juniper, and for dry eczema we recommend geranium and lavender.

General advice It is well known that eczema responds well to a cleansing diet. This means eating lots of fruit and vegetables, avoiding meat and dairy products, and drinking plenty of mineral water.

Prematurely Aged Skin

This may be due to a variety of different reasons, including illness, a sudden loss of weight, climatic conditions, excessive sunbathing or pure neglect. Skin can look much older than the actual age of the person. Excessive dryness accentuates lines and causes the neck tissue to become crêpey and the muscles to droop. The answer here is to concentrate on helping the skin to get back some of its former tonicity and elasticity and feeding the tissues to give them back some hydration.

Cleansing We recommend a nourishing and tonifying cleansing milk containing rose, ylang ylang or patchouli. Good lotions include rose water, orange blossom water and Evian spray. It is also possible to put grapes, apples or raspberries in a juice extractor and to use the resultant juice on the face.

Face oil We recommend 3 per cent essential oil of either basil, geranium, marjoram, patchouli, rose or rosemary in either jojoba or wheatgerm vegetable oil.

Face mask It is advisable to use a mask that helps to tighten the skin. Try, for example, camphor, or clay powder mixed with water and one drop only of essential oil of patchouli or geranium. Use at least one of these each week.

General advice Check your general health and make sure you are eating a healthy diet and getting plenty of vitamins. Take the time to relax – and if you smoke, give it up!

Very Dehydrated Skin
This is usually the result of either internal problems, such as illness – especially of the liver – or external factors, such as excessive exposure to the sun. Whatever the cause, the skin needs to be revitalized.

Cleansing Use a nourishing cleansing milk, such as neroli or patchouli. Good lotions include orange blossom water and apple or cucumber juice made with a juice extractor.

Face oil We recommend 3 per cent essential oil of neroli, patchouli, rose and sandalwood in jojoba or wheatgerm vegetable oil.

Face mask A weekly mask using slices of cucumber should help. A herbal gel mask is very soothing.

General advice Avoid highly spiced food, smoking and overexposure to wind or sun. Do not sit too near an open fire.

Plastic Surgery
Essential oils are very useful when a client has had plastic surgery.
  A skin that has been prepared in advance with essential oils always gets better results in any surgery. Wounds and cuts heal more quickly, the formation of scar tissue is minimal, and the production of vigorous new

cells is speeded up. In the case of plastic surgery of the nose, which is one of the most common operations, the bruising disperses much more quickly. Essential oils are so highly antiseptic that they keep the tissues healthy and stop any secondary infection.

We recommend using essential oils both before and after surgery. An individual formula is always preferable, but generally a face oil made up of 3 per cent essential oils of juniper, lavender and neroli in jojoba vegetable oil is very successful. Essential oils are more effective if used immediately after the scars have formed, though the oil should then be applied only around the scar until a scab has formed. They can also help old scar tissue, though the process is then rather slower.

ELECTROLYSIS

Some of our clients have electrolysis for the removal of superfluous hair. Essential oils such as lavender and camomile are very beneficial in these cases, thanks to their great antiseptic properties. At the same time, their soothing and healing action helps to control both inflammation and any slight scarring that may occasionally occur.

AROMATIC CREAMS

Some skins, particularly highly sensitive and mature ones, require more protection than others; some require more protection under stressful conditions, such as cold weather with strong winds. With all this in mind, we have created a range of aromatic creams. These have a similar formulation to face oils, but with the difference that we use beeswax as a binding agent. This allows the cream to stay on the surface of the skin for longer, where it forms a thin coating and offers a better protection.

Many of our clients use face oil for everyday use, and the cream when external conditions demand it.

BODY PRODUCTS

These are useful both for maintaining a good quality skin and for treating specific problems. They include body oils and bath oils.

Body oils

We have seen how beneficial essential oils can be to many skin conditions on the face, and the same is largely true of the body. Many of the same problems that affect the face can also affect the body.

These include excessively dry or oily skins, infected, sensitive, allergic and acidic skins. Poor blood circulation, particularly on the feet, legs and sometimes on the hands, gives a mauve, marbled appearance to the skin. There can be infiltration of fluid and fat. Premature ageing of the skin can be caused by illness or excessive sunbathing. And muscle contraction can be brought on by excessive tension or over-vigorous exercise.

Our body oils are made with 2 to 5 per cent essential oils, depending on the condition and the strength of the essence used, in a vegetable oil. We usually put three or four different essential oils in a preparation.

Body oil should be applied very lightly, as a little goes a long way. It can be applied in the morning, at least 15 minutes before dressing, or at night, either after a bath or on its own.

Bath oils

Baths have been taken since time immemorial to improve both health and looks. Continuing in this tradition, bath oils, in which essential oils are used, are the most popular of our preparations.

An aromatic bath is not only useful for the wonderful aroma it creates, but also for the numerous therapeutic properties in the various essential oils. It is magical to relax at night in a warm bath. Morning baths, using uplifting and fortifying essential oils, are also excellent.

Essential oils are not absorbed by water, so they form droplets that will stay on the surface. Even if they are mixed into the water, they still have a tendency to stay on the surface. Their therapeutic action is gained through breathing in the odoriferous molecules they produce.

Simply place 4 to 6 drops of essential oil in the bathwater. Always check the properties of the essential oil before using it in the bath, as some can be an irritant to the skin.

Some manufacturers use a special disperser that allows the essential oil to be more evenly mixed into the water. In this case, their action is beneficial both by their aroma and by osmosis through the skin into the bloodstream.

The temperature of the bath and the length of time spent in it are also important. Spending 15 to 20 minutes in a warm bath is calming. A cooler bath is invigorating. Very hot baths are not good for the vascular system and are not advised in cases of varicose veins, thread veins, hemorrhoids, high blood pressure, cardiac problems and pregnancy.

Too many baths have a drying effect on the skin and diminish its protection against infection. Aromatic baths, on the other hand, help to preserve and restore the skin. Four aromatic baths a week is the usual recommendation, except when otherwise prescribed.

A point to take note of when having a bath; do not rub your hands on your eyes in case they have some of the essential oil on them.

Foot-baths

Aromatic foot-baths are highly effective and are often prescribed when it is difficult, for whatever reason, to have a full bath. Use just 2 to 3 drops of essential oil, mix well into the water and soak for 10 to 15 minutes. This method is useful for people who prefer taking showers to baths.

HAND CARE

Hands are very important and, if they are not taken care of, can give away the age of a person even more than the face and neck. We use our hands for so many daily chores that, if we are not careful to protect and nourish them, they can soon take on a very poor condition.

Even the best quality skin quickly suffers from so much contact with detergents and other household products. And much as gardening is a wonderful occupation, it has a harmful effect on the hands unless they are well protected.

Bearing in mind the constant ill-use that the hands receive, we have created a special treatment for their care in our clinic. We use a deep, soothing massage with a special oil, made with essential oils of patchouli, which is good for keeping the tissues well nourished, and lemon, which is excellent for the quality of the skin, both softening and whitening it. These essences are mixed at 3 per cent with either wheatgerm vegetable oil, which is high in vitamin E, or jojoba vegetable oil, which is excellent for feeding the skin. If there has been any problem with burns, essential oil of lavender can be added to the mixture.

We also apply a warm poultice made with crushed linseed. This can be bought in health shops either ready crushed or whole, in which case you can crush it yourself in a coffee grinder. The linseed oil is good for the skin, and the added warmth encourages the penetration of the oil more deeply into the skin. The feeling on the hands is unbelievably soothing and comforting, and immediately improves the quality of the skin. It is particularly helpful in cases of rheumatism and arthritic joints. It also improves both the blood circulation and the lymph flow, so making the hands more supple and less prone to aches and pains. The same treatment is helpful after injuries.

For home care, we recommend applying the specially prepared oil, as given above, morning and night. It should be massaged well into the skin, while smoothing each finger with a movement similar to that of putting on gloves. Give your hands a bath, with two drops of essential oil of either lavender or lemon well mixed into a bowl of warm water, at least four times a week.

NAIL CARE

The nails are taken care of as part of any hand treatment, but if they need more attention you can use an oil made with 2 per cent essential oil of lemon and lavender in jojoba, almond or wheatgerm vegetable oil. This oil must be well massaged into the nail area, particularly around the cuticles, for a few minutes morning and night.

FOOT CARE

Feet, which daily carry our weight and are often put into ill-fitting shoes, have even greater problems than hands. The same treatment as that recommended for the hands will have marvellous results.

HAIR CARE

We have created a special hair oil to improve blood circulation on the scalp. It promotes hair growth, nourishes the hair and makes it look shinier. It also acts as a regulator of excessive dryness or oiliness.

For fair hair, the oil is made up with 2 per cent essential oils of bay, camomile and sage in jojoba vegetable oil, or half castor and half soya vegetable oils. For dark hair, it is made with 2 per cent essential oils of bay, rosemary and sage in jojoba vegetable oil, or half castor and half soya vegetable oils.

The oil must be well massaged into the scalp, using circular movements and ending with a movement of the hands from the roots to the hair ends. It should be applied a few hours before shampooing, or the night before (in which case you should put a towel on the pillow). The hair is then shampooed. This should be repeated every seven to 14 days.

Menstrual Problems

Menstruation has not always been something that people felt they could talk about. Many societies and cultures have considered menstruating women to be in some way unclean and thus taboo. And in ancient times, it was never mentioned in polite society, and certainly not in front of men.

Menstruation has often been described in terms that are most unfair to this very necessary and perfectly normal female function. The word 'curse', for example, suggests that menstruation is highly undesirable. The modern approach, however, is a very different one. There is great freedom of expression nowadays on both sexual matters and female functions.

Normally, menstrual periods do not cause many problems. Occasionally, however, they can be accompanied by discomforts and changes of mood, though these are not usually bad enough to interfere with daily life.

PREMENSTRUAL SYNDROME

One of the most common problems associated with menstruation is known as premenstrual syndrome or, more commonly, premenstrual tension.

This term covers a group of physical, emotional and mental changes, which begin between two and 14 days before menstruation and are usually relieved once it has started. It can vary from very slight, barely noticeable reactions to severe ones that can, in extreme cases, require medical attention.

The symptoms are numerous and affect different women in different ways. The most common include a swollen abdomen, weight gain, painful breasts, pain or cramp in the abdomen or lower back, low urine output, headaches, skin eruptions, irritability, tension, depression, lethargy, reduced powers of concentration, loss of confidence, absence of sex drive, change in appetite, craving for certain foods and irrational behaviour.

WHAT CAN AROMATHERAPY DO?

The first thing we do when a client comes to see us suffering from premenstrual tension is to assess her background, her tensions, her temperament and her medical history. We are then able to determine a programme, based on our findings, to counteract the situation. Aromatherapy treatments are very helpful for this problem. Working on various nerve points helps to stimulate and regulate the nervous system. Some pressure points linked to the endocrine system stimulate the different glands into functioning better. It is helpful, too, for the therapist to concentrate on lymphatic drainage – especially in the lumbar area, where most of the congestion and fluid retention is concentrated – as this releases tension and helps eliminate impurities and any excessive build-up of fluid.

Essential oils

For the massage, we use any of the following essential oils: basil, cypress, camomile, cajuput, juniper, peppermint, lavender, rose, rosemary, sage and thyme, mixed with vegetable oils of sesame, jojoba, soya or wheatgerm.

It is important to have regular treatments – ideally weekly to start with, then gradually becoming monthly. You should always try to have a treatment within the 10 days before a period is due to start, as this is usually when problems begin.

Self-help

Take five aromatic baths a week, alternating between sage, lavender, rosemary, juniper and camomile. Use a body oil made of lavender, rosemary and geranium in wheatgerm oil and, for the face, a camomile oil in jojoba oil.

A great many herb teas are helpful for all kinds of menstrual problems. For example, dandelion and rosemary are good for fluid retention; marjoram is calming and good for the digestion; camomile is decongestive; raspberry leaf relieves pain; thyme regulates periods; lavender is calming; sage is excellent if there is a tendency to heavy periods; parsley and rose are recommended if periods are late; uva ursi has a diuretic effect; and ash leaf is a good general cleanser.

Regular exercise is beneficial. Yoga is particularly good, as it helps to release tension and works on the lumbar area to prevent cramp and the overall congestive state.

A balanced diet – preferably vegetarian – helps to keep the digestive and intestinal tracts in good condition. To supplement this, there are several good products on the market in the form of special vitamins and minerals for women, with emphasis on the B vitamins, especially B6, Dolomite (calcium and magnesium) and vitamin E (which is not recommended, however, for anyone suffering from high blood pressure).

It is also worth trying to minimize the constant little irritations of most people's daily lives. To this end, it is a good idea to talk to your family, to ask them to be careful not to provoke any tense or unpleasant situations and to give you a chance to work through your problem.

With care and understanding, the symptoms can nearly always be much improved fairly rapidly and will, in time, probably disappear altogether. If, however, the premenstrual tension is severe, you should consult your doctor.

OTHER MENSTRUAL PROBLEMS
Some women have no periods at all, or have them only occasionally. They may have had this problem ever since puberty, in which case it can come from an imbalance in the endocrine system.

There are other women who experience a shock or emotional trauma which affects the nervous system to such an extent that menstruation stops temporarily or for long periods of time. Anorectics can be affected in this way, as can women on the contraceptive pill.

Massage is the same as for premenstrual tension, again working particularly on the lumbar region where the problem is largely centred. The essential oils of sage, juniper, camomile, basil, lavender, rosemary and thyme should be used, both in the clinic and for home care in the form of body and bath oils.

Heavy periods
In the case of very heavy periods, we give a lighter treatment, using the essential oil of rose, which is a good regulator of the menstrual cycle; lavender, which is calming; neroli, which is good for the nervous system; camomile and lemon, both of which help to prevent anemia, as this can result from a heavy loss of blood; and sage, which is a good regulator. The massage is beneficial in re-establishing equilibrium to the body as a whole.

It is important to rest as much as possible and it is advisable to consult a medical practitioner if the condition worsens. For home care, take four lavender baths a week; use a body oil made with camomile, rose and ylang ylang in wheatgerm or jojoba vegetable oil; drink herb teas of camomile, marjoram and thyme; and eat a good, balanced diet.

The Menopause – a Second Beginning?

~~~

There is no health subject more misunderstood and ridiculed than the menopause. It happens to every woman, yet it is treated like some sort of strange, mysterious state which is mentioned only in hushed tones. To listen to some people, you would think that this was the end of the poor woman as a feminine human being.

Is it not possible to find a more positive term for this transitory period in a woman's life than 'change of life'? I suggest 'the second beginning', because it is exactly that. It is not an illness. It is rather a readjustment of the endocrine balance in the body.

WHEN DOES IT HAPPEN?

This second beginning usually starts when a woman is in her late forties or early fifties – though it can happen much earlier, in the mid to late thirties, or much later, in the mid fifties.

Each woman has her own rhythm, depending on hereditary factors, climate, diet, way of life, environment and general health. However, with the increasing stresses of modern life, there is a tendency these days for the menopause to manifest itself earlier rather than later.

WHAT TO EXPECT

It is important to realize that the change does not happen in one day. We always tell our clients that the gradual onset is a good thing because it is nature's way of sending us warning signals of the impending transition and of all the deficiencies that can occur during the main phase of the change. We often have to help the client to challenge her negative attitude to this phase of her life.

Nor does it affect all women in the same way. In order to complete its cycle, the endocrine system must follow its own individual pattern. No two people are alike. The same – or at least similar – symptoms are often experienced by women of the same family, which is explained both by hereditary factors and by their coming from a similar physical and emotional environment.

SYMPTOMS

For simplicity, the symptoms that many women experience during the menopause can be grouped under eight different categories.

These are:

- ⚺ hot flushes, congestive state, excessive sweating
- ⚺ high blood pressure
- ⚺ low blood pressure
- ⚺ palpitations
- ⚺ anemia
- ⚺ depression, irritability, moodiness
- ⚺ scanty or heavy periods
- ⚺ weight increase, fluid retention, bloating

Let us look at each category in turn, and examine both what can happen and what can be done to remedy the situation.

HOT FLUSHES, CONGESTIVE STATE, EXCESSIVE SWEATING

Women often complain of hot flushes, best described as excessive blushing, which can be more or less severe. Their cause is not known. They seem to happen when the menopause has already started, and they could be linked with the change in the production of estrogen. They are quite harmless, if unpleasant.

What you can do

- ⚺ Avoid extreme and sudden changes of temperature. Keep out of strong, cold winds and avoid too much sunshine.
- ⚺ Avoid emotional upsets and confined spaces.
- ⚺ Do not have any stimulating drinks, such as alcohol, coffee or tea (other than China tea) and avoid drinks that are too hot.
- ⚺ Certain herb teas can help, such as sage, lime blossom, camomile and peppermint.
- ⚺ Use only gentle and soothing products on the skin. Evian spray is very useful to decongest the tissues and to bring relief if you have a feeling of excessive heat.
- ⚺ Avoid eating spicy food, meat, sugar and food that is too hot.
- ⚺ Vitamin supplements can be useful. Try vitamins C, E and B complex and Dolomite (calcium and magnesium).
- ⚺ Refrain from smoking, which encourages a congestive state.
- ⚺ Hot flushes are sometimes accompanied by sweating, especially at night. This does not necessarily affect the whole body, but may be localized to the head and feet, for example. It is difficult to accept that this helps to cleanse the system, but it is in fact true.
- ⚺ Gentle exercise is good, but do not embark on anything too strenuous.

Recommended aromatherapy treatments

- ⚺ Facial compresses of camomile lotion, witch-hazel, rose water or orange blossom water.

✗ A calming and decongestive face oil, with 1–2 per cent essential oil in jojoba, wheatgerm or St John's wort vegetable oil. The best essential oils to use are camomile, neroli, rose, sandalwood, and geranium in low dosage.

✗ The essential oil of camomile. Congestive states can lead to broken capillaries, especially on the face but sometimes also on the body. Great care is required, therefore, in protection and prevention. The essential oil of camomile is excellent, either mixed with a vegetable oil such as jojoba or wheatgerm or in a beeswax preparation for better protection. Any cream made with azulene, a camomile extract, is very beneficial. Essential oils of sandalwood and rose can be used in the same way.

✗ A body oil using soothing essential oils, such as camomile, neroli, rose, sandalwood and geranium, with peppermint added for its cooling effect. We suggest 2 to 4 per cent essential oil in soya vegetable oil.

✗ A bath oil four times a week, using essential oils of either lavender, which is relaxing; or geranium, which is invigorating and good for the circulation; or sandalwood, which is good for fluid retention. Make sure that the water is not too hot, or it could have quite the wrong effect.

✗ A clay foot-bath four times a week, using one large tablespoon of clay powder well mixed into a bowl of warm water, to drain impurities away from the system. Soak the feet for 10 to 15 minutes.

HIGH BLOOD PRESSURE

Depending on the severity of the case, we usually refer the client to a doctor. Sometimes the client is prone to anger and frustration, which create just the right conditions for high blood pressure. Dealing with this is not so much a question of making radical changes in your way of life as learning how to cope with things as they are. Nobody is perfect, and it is important to recognize and accept your shortcomings.

What you can do

✗ Stress has a bad effect on the system and often leads to high blood pressure. It is important, therefore, not to drive yourself too hard, and to relax as much as possible.

✗ Try to avoid arguing: it is better to avoid any situation that can cause anger and frustration than to risk raising your blood pressure.

✗ High blood pressure can cause a highly congested state, and it is advisable to follow a light cleansing diet containing plenty of fruit and vegetables and to avoid spirits, smoking, any rich or spicy food, meat and too much salt.

✗ Garlic is good for high blood pressure.

✗ Rutin (which is derived from buckwheat) and evening primrose oil are both helpful, but check with your doctor if you are on any medication.

Recommended aromatherapy treatments

✗ Any of the calming essential oils and those that are helpful to the blood circulation in face, body and bath oils. Suitable essential oils include basil, camomile, geranium, lavender, neroli and sandalwood.

If the client has very high blood pressure, the therapist will ask her to check with her doctor before having aromatherapy treatment. If the doctor agrees to it, the treatment should not be too long or too deep, the emphasis being on relaxation.

Low Blood Pressure

Low blood pressure is fairly common among women and must be treated with care. The therapist will often allow the client to lie with a small cushion under her head and will be very careful not to let her get up too quickly from the couch as this can bring on dizziness and, in extreme cases, can even cause her to faint.

What you can do

✗ Take walks in the fresh air, but do not exhaust yourself.
✗ Do everything in moderation.
✗ Follow a good, fortifying diet, with plenty of protein, fruit and vegetables, and try a general multi-vitamin and mineral supplement.

Recommended aromatherapy treatments

✗ A face oil made up of a base of jojoba oil and 3 per cent essential oil of patchouli, rose and sandalwood, plus one drop of geranium to pep up the mixture. People with low blood pressure often suffer from a very dry skin, and are usually quite pale. This face oil is very helpful.
✗ A fortifying body oil, with 4 per cent geranium, ylang ylang and lavender in jojoba or wheatgerm vegetable oil.
✗ A relaxing bath oil, using lavender or geranium.

Palpitations

Palpitations are usually caused by nervous reactions.

What you can do

✗ Get as much rest as possible.
✗ Try to understand your nervous system and to judge what it is that causes this overreaction, so that you can avoid exposing yourself to it.

Recommended aromatherapy treatments

✗ Essential oils that are good for the nervous system, such as lavender, neroli, petitgrain and vetivert, are good in body oils, both in the clinic and for home care.
✗ Relaxing baths of lavender, or rosemary which is a cardiac regulator.

ANEMIA

Anemia affects many women at this period of their lives, especially if they have a tendency to lose a lot of blood during menstruation. If the anemia is serious the therapist will recommend that the client seeks a medical opinion.

What you can do

- Iron tablets are not suitable for everyone and can cause constipation. Molasses is a good substitute.
- A good fortifying diet is recommended, with plenty of protein, fruit and vegetables. Vitamin supplements are helpful.
- Get plenty of rest.

Recommended aromatherapy treatments

- A face oil using 3 per cent essential oils of rose, which is an excellent regulator of the endocrine system, and ylang ylang, which has an uplifting effect, in jojoba or wheatgerm vegetable oil. Add just one drop each of geranium and jasmine to pep up the mixture.
- A body oil using 4 per cent essential oils of ylang ylang and rose in calendula vegetable oil.
- A bath oil using essential oil of lavender, which is very relaxing.

The treatment should not be too deep. The aim is to regulate the system and stimulate the blood circulation.

DEPRESSION, IRRITABILITY, MOODINESS

Women who have a tendency to be depressive may become more so during this period of hormonal change. The ones who are usually optimistic may still be affected, but probably only slightly and temporarily.

A lot of women who have devoted their lives to their families feel, when their children leave home, that their lives are suddenly empty. This can be a major contributing factor in feelings of depression at this time.

Women tend to feel more fragile, more sensitive and more vulnerable at this time of life. Nature is telling the body that it is time to slow down and to avoid stress.

What you can do

- Relieve black moods and feelings of anger and frustration by concentrating on outside interests. Try taking exercise, such as going for walks; taking up a new sport (though nothing too strenuous); trying your hand at a new hobby; or playing a part in voluntary work.
- If you are confused by ambivalent feelings, try putting them down on paper in order to clarify things in your mind.
- Think positive and look on the bright side. It is a great luxury to live at your own rhythm – so enjoy it!

❊ Now is the time to get closer to your partner. You might even like to organize a second honeymoon!

❊ Try not to take any strong drugs. These often bring out personality changes and it sometimes becomes difficult to stop taking them.

❊ If your sleep is disturbed, sleeping pills are not the answer. Take a look at your bedtime routine and see what you can do to facilitate sleep. For example, do not take too stimulating a drink before retiring, such as coffee or white wine, but try a herb tea, such as camomile, lime blossom, melissa or passiflora. Take a short walk before going to bed. Do not indulge in any mental activity that might be too stimulating and choose your reading matter for its ability to relax, not excite.

Recommended aromatherapy treatments

❊ A drop of essential oil of vetivert or neroli on your handkerchief under the pillow.

❊ A relaxing bath before bed, with an essential oil of lavender or petitgrain.

SCANTY OR HEAVY PERIODS

Scanty periods that gradually disappear are a blessing.

Heavy periods, on the other hand, are more of a problem – not only physically, because they drain energy and can cause anemia, but also emotionally, because of a lowered physical resistance. They can be caused by fibroids.

What you can do if you have heavy periods

❊ A medical check-up is advisable.

❊ Make sure you are getting plenty of rest.

Recommended aromatherapy treatments

❊ Massage, which will undoubtedly help but should not be too deep.

❊ Essential oils of lavender and rosemary in body and bath oils.

WEIGHT INCREASE, FLUID RETENTION, BLOATING

A certain amount of fluid retention is bound to affect women at this time. Bloating often occurs, which can be a very uncomfortable feeling. There are, however, certain things that will help.

What you can do

❊ A vegetarian diet is best, with plenty of diuretic fruit and vegetables, such as celery, onions, leeks, grapes and melon.

❊ Try drinking herb teas such as dandelion, uva ursi and sage, all of which have a naturally diuretic effect.

✕ It is best not to take any fluid with meals. Avoid spirits and coffee.
✕ Kelp tablets are excellent fluid regulators.

Recommended aromatherapy treatments

✕ A body oil made up of 4 per cent essential oils of lavender, sage, rosemary and geranium in soya vegetable oil. This will improve and stimulate blood circulation and lymph flow.
✕ Aromatic baths of lavender and rosemary. These will complement the work already done by the body oil.
✕ A face oil containing 3 per cent essential oils of sandalwood, basil and rose in jojoba vegetable oil.

In Conclusion

Menopausal women often feel that they are greatly helped by aromatherapy treatments. They not only feel physically better, they gain courage from the support they receive from the therapist and this, in turn, encourages them to take better care of themselves.

To end on an optimistic note, there is an increasing number of women who remain feminine and glamorous, active and successful at this time of their lives; living proof of a positive second beginning.

One Woman's Experience . . .

Miss J had been a keen advocate of aromatherapy for many years. In her early fifties, she had put on nearly 2 stone during her menopause, and was therefore very keen to lose weight. She was equally keen, however, to do this sensibly.

With four clear weeks at her disposal, free of any commitments from a busy and highly stressed job, aromatherapy seemed to be the best approach for her. She therefore embarked on a course of aromatherapy treatments aimed specifically at losing weight.

She met regularly, twice a week, with a therapist whom she found to be highly sensitive and sympathetic. Her therapist gave her not only aromatherapy massage but also a lot of much needed and welcome encouragement to continue with both her balanced reducing diet and her exercise programme. This greatly strengthened her resolve.

At the end of the month, Miss J felt not only relaxed but, at the same time, stimulated, revitalized and uplifted, with all batteries recharged. The physical and mental tension that had been getting her down before seemed to have flown out of the window.

With the help of her therapist, she had succeeded in developing an excellent home-care routine, and this she was able to continue long after her course of treatments in the clinic had finished. All in all, she was absolutely delighted with the results.

Overweight

In ancient times, excess weight was considered to be a mark of wealth and status. Today it is recognized as a major problem. Certain cultures still accept it, but our western society does not. The media and the medical profession leave us in no doubt that it is unhealthy and unsightly.

Overweight is a result of excess fat or fluid, or both. It goes from a few extra pounds to obesity, which is an increase of between 20 and 30 per cent of normal weight.

There are several different reasons for being overweight, each of which we shall examine in turn.

FLUID RETENTION

This is the classic case of the 'sponge woman'. Women affected in this way are usually shapely, feminine types, producing more feminine hormones in their bodies. The excessive amount of water in the tissues can happen at any age, but is more accentuated at the beginning of the menstrual cycle and at the menopause.

Aromatherapy treatment has many movements that work to improve lymphatic drainage, which is very effective in helping to control fluid retention. Stress has the effect of diminishing blood circulation and lymphatic drainage so, by contrast, all movements which promote relaxation will increase the benefits of the massage.

The massage must therefore be deep and relaxing, as well as stimulating the system to function better. We use face and body oils containing diuretic essential oils, such as cypress, juniper, lavender, lemon, rosemary, sage, sandalwood and thyme.

Body oils and bath products using the same essential oils should be used at home to carry on the work done during the clinic treatment. Overwork makes the condition worse and rest is therefore very important. Gentle exercise, such as short walks in fresh air, is helpful.

We recommend clients to check their diet and to refrain from using too much salt and from drinking alcohol, as both encourage fluid retention. It is best to avoid drinking with meals. Some fruit and vegetables – notably strawberries, melon, grapes, pineapple, celery and leeks – are highly diuretic. Herb teas that have a diuretic effect include ash leaf, burdock, cherry stalks, dandelion and uva ursi.

INFILTRATION OF FAT

This is caused not only by an excessive amount of food, but often by the wrong kind of food and a bad combination of nutrients. When we are dealing with a client who is being treated medically and is following a specific diet, we do not interfere with this. Otherwise, we give recommendations for a healthy way of eating.

When a client does not feel strong enough to follow the diet on her own and needs the support of a group, we advise her to join Weight Watchers. It is undoubtedly easier for many women to diet when they are encouraged by being part of a group and are monitored on a regular basis. In cases of extreme obesity and if the client is not already under medical supervision, we advise her to see her doctor.

When a client is excessively overweight it is difficult to work on the pressure points on the back, because of excess fat in the tissues. We concentrate instead on reflex points on the feet and head, and on accessible lymph points. The massage must be deep and slow, using essential oils of juniper, lemon, orange, rosemary, rose or sage. The rebalancing of the system encourages it to function better and helps speed up the metabolic rate.

Home care involves body oils and bath products made up of the same essential oils as in the clinic. It is important to have weekly treatments when losing weight, because the tissues have a tendency to sag; massage helps this and to tone the muscles. We also recommend gentle exercise classes.

Herb teas are an added help. In particular, we recommend ash leaf, which is a good intestinal cleanser; dandelion, which acts on the kidneys; and sage, which works on the endocrine system.

Nervous Origin

This kind of excess weight usually happens after a traumatic experience, such as a great shock, a bereavement or a serious illness, leading to an emotional imbalance. Treatment must both calm and, at the same time, stimulate the nervous system.

The overall emphasis of the massage is on relaxation. Movements that help to rebalance the energy field create a release of tension. The massage must not be too deep, as the nervous system could not take it. The essential oils we use for this treatment are chosen for their calming and regulating effects on the nervous system, including basil, camomile, lavender, marjoram, neroli, orange, tangerine, vetivert, and ylang ylang.

For home care, we suggest body oils and bath products using the same essential oils as in the clinic. We also advise applying one drop only of vetivert or marjoram in an anti-clockwise direction on the solar plexus, morning and night. A diet rich in aromats, particularly sage, rosemary, parsley, basil, marjoram and thyme, is helpful to stimulate bile flow and to rebalance the digestive tract. Herb teas that can be very helpful include camomile, skullcap, lime blossom, lemon verbena and melissa.

Generally speaking it is difficult to achieve a result for this condition without the help of psychotherapy. Many people use their fat as a sort of protection and cannot take it off until they have resolved whatever it was that made them put it on in the first place.

An Imbalance of the Endocrine System

Dysfunction of the endocrine system can cause an increase in weight. The problem can be aggravated at certain times, such as at the time of the menopause.

The massage is deep, slow and relaxing, with emphasis on movements that speed up the blood circulation and that work on nerve points related to the endocrine system. We use essential oils of cypress, geranium, lavender, rose, rosemary, sage and ylang ylang.

We give the client products for home care, including body and bath oils containing the same essential oils as those used in the clinic. We also recommend a herb tea, such as sage, which is especially good for this condition.

Hereditary Factors

Hereditary factors can predispose a person to a weight problem, and a look at the person's family background often shows the same tendency for many members of the same family. This may be caused by inherited genes, though more often than not it is caused by the same pattern of living, such as poor diet and lack of exercise. In consultation with the client, we assess the situation and then follow either the programme for fluid retention or the programme for infiltration of fat.

Leg Care

Beautiful legs are every woman's dream. Problems with your legs can not only make them less attractive but can also sometimes be quite painful.

Legorama

In our clinic we have created a complete treatment, which we call legorama. This is tailored to the requirements of the individual client, depending on the particular condition of her legs. It consists of 10 treatments, preferably twice weekly.

Each treatment lasts for an hour and comprises a highly specialized leg massage, using particular blends of essential oils that are good for the circulation, for lymphatic drainage and for skin texture. These include cypress, which is good for the veins; juniper, which has an excellent purifying effect; geranium, which is toning and good for the blood circulation; lavender, which is diuretic and eases aches and pains as well as being good for the texture of the skin; rosemary, which is good for stiffness, muscle fatigue and fluid retention; sandalwood, which is diuretic and toning, as well as having a gentle and soothing effect on the skin; sage, which is good for the endocrine system; and thyme, which is a powerful antiseptic and is good for aches and pains, and for fluid retention.

The use of clay

The other aspect of the treatment is the use of clay compresses. This means that compresses are steeped in clay lotion, which is reinforced by essential oils, and these are applied directly to the legs.

Clay has invaluable therapeutic properties and has been used since ancient times to treat many ills. It is a rich earth of oily consistency and can be green, red, grey or white. It is a living substance, which fights germs and helps in the formation of healthy cells.

Like essential oils, it is highly antiseptic. It has a tremendous power of absorption – so much so, in fact, that body toxins are drawn to the area being treated. It also deodorizes and protects against radiation.

In the clay lotion, we use two different essential oils – either geranium or peppermint. The geranium is toning, healing and astringent, which is good for varicosity, as well as being good for the blood circulation; while the peppermint is antiseptic, astringent, cooling and soothing.

Contra-indications

If you are under medical treatment of any kind you should seek your doctor's advice before having this treatment, particularly if you are pregnant, have just had a baby or have recently had an operation. If any of your leg conditions are in an advanced, serious stage, you should, in any case, consult your doctor.

HOME CARE

As with any other treatment, success relies on regular treatments, plus a follow-up at home using specially prepared products. Home treatment should not be carried out on the same day as treatment received at the clinic.

Body oils

Spread the oil evenly all over the legs. Sit up and work firmly up and down the legs using a massage movement, crossing the hands backwards and forwards. Lying down, massage the legs as if you were putting on stockings, from foot to thigh.

Lotions

Use either peppermint or geranium clay lotion, or a plain clay lotion made up of 1 teaspoon of clay powder to 1 glass of water. Use old stockings, wrung out in water and then soaked in the lotion. Put these on and then sit or lie down with the legs raised and leave for one hour, or until the stockings are dry.

Bath oils

Soak in the bath for 10 to 15 minutes. Never take too hot a bath, especially if you have varicose veins, as very hot water can aggravate the condition.

WHAT PRODUCT FOR WHAT CONDITION?

The product is chosen carefully, according to the client's condition. We advise that, when the course of treatments has been completed and all the products for home care are finished, the client should contact the therapist before undertaking another course or replacing the products.

Heavy, aching legs

These are due to poor blood circulation, which often results in cold feet and blue or mauve legs.

In the morning, apply a body oil made up of essential oils of cypress, geranium, sandalwood and sage in soya bean vegetable oil to both legs. Massage in well.

In the evening, alternate between a lavender bath, a rosemary bath and plain clay lotion compresses. Finish by massaging geranium body oil all over the body.

Swollen ankles and feet

These are due to excessive infiltration of fat or, more often, to fluid retention.

In the morning, massage the legs with a body oil, made up of a mixture of geranium, rosemary and sandalwood in soya bean vegetable oil.

In the evening, alternate between a rosemary bath, plain clay lotion compresses, a sage bath and peppermint clay lotion compresses. Finish by massaging rosemary body oil all over the body.

Thread veins and varicose veins

These are caused by the fragility of the veins and by poor blood circulation.

In the morning, gently apply to the legs a body oil made up of essential oils of cypress, geranium, lavender and rosemary in soya bean vegetable oil.

In the evening, alternate between a sage bath, geranium clay lotion compresses, a rosemary bath and plain clay lotion compresses. Finish by applying geranium body oil all over the body.

Discoloured patches on the legs

These are due to many factors, such as ulceration, burns and poor blood circulation.

In the morning, alternate between using sandalwood body oil and juniper body oil. Massage into the legs.

In the evening, alternate between a lavender bath, plain clay lotion compresses, a sage bath and peppermint clay lotion compresses. Finish alternately with juniper body oil or sandalwood body oil and massage all over the body.

Chilblains

Chilblains are an inflamed condition of the skin. They are generally found on the feet, but can also occur on the hands. They are due to a number of things, including defective circulation, a lack of vitamins and a poor state of general health.

In the morning, apply thyme and lavender body oil all over the legs.

In the evening, alternate between a pine bath, pine body oil, a lavender bath and geranium body oil. After a bath, finish by applying geranium body oil all over the body.

GENERAL ADVICE

Do not sit with your legs crossed as this interferes with blood circulation. Avoid excessive changes of temperature and sunbathing, specially where varicose veins are concerned. Wear woollen tights when the weather is very cold. Sleep with your feet slightly raised, and put your feet up as often as possible during the day. Do not wear tight clothing or footwear, as they would impede both the circulation and lymph flow.

Exercise

Regular exercise, such as walking and swimming, is beneficial. Walking in the sea up to your ankles is particularly good as this provides an excellent massage. Gentle cycling, dancing and gymnastic movements are all recommended for the various conditions that can affect the legs in any of the ways described above.

Diet

Follow a sensible diet, low in fats and sugars, high in fresh fruit and vegetables. Too much protein can cause excessive acidity. Eat slowly and chew well.

Try to drink at least one cup a day of herb tea when following the treatments. For swollen feet, ankles and legs, drink diuretic teas such as dandelion, uva ursi, cherry stalks and ash leaf. For varicose veins, poor blood circulation and chilblains, drink thyme, hawthorn, lavender and lemon juice. Take vitamins C and P, which reinforce the quality of the vessel walls; rutin tablets and vitamin E, both of which improve the circulation.

CELLULITIS

This is a dysfunction in the cellular tissue. Lymphatic drainage is usually poor, in which case there may be infiltration of toxic materials, making it a painful condition. The tissues can feel either hard or soft to the touch. The skin takes on the spongy appearance of orange peel.

It is usually localized, most commonly on the thighs, but can also be found on other parts of the body, such as the arms and tops of the shoulders. This condition can happen at any age, regardless of weight; and can affect even very slim people.

Cellulitis can be caused by many factors. These include a weak liver; a general intoxication of the system because of poor nutrition, overwork, emotional upset, stress or lack of exercise; an imbalance in the endocrine system; or ovarian disfunction as, for example, in the menopause.

What you can do

We recommend clients to follow a detoxifying diet – avoiding meat, condiments such as salt, pepper, mustard and so on, fried foods, sauces, fermented cheese, smoked and salty foods, sugar, cakes, pastries and sweets. Avoid alcoholic and sweet drinks and instead take diuretic and cleansing herb teas such as ash leaf, dandelion and uva ursi, which will help the system to eliminate waste materials.

How aromatherapy can help

We have devised a specific treatment for this condition. In order for it to work effectively, we recommend a minimum of two treatments a week for five weeks.

The treatment consists of a body massage involving the lower part of the torso from the waist down, the legs and feet. The therapist applies essential oils that detoxify, help the lymphatic tract and speed up the blood circulation. These include cypress, lavender, lemon, orange, sage and tangerine. The degree of pressure of the massage movements is determined by the kind of cellulitis concerned and the sensitivity of the tissues. The therapist then applies poultices of crushed linseed on infiltrated areas to help the penetration of essential oils and to help drain away toxic materials.

Home care involves body oil and bath products made up with the same essential oils as those used in the clinic treatments. It is important for the client to relax and to rest as much as possible in order to give the system the chance to regain its balance. We also recommend client's to take gentle exercise classes.

Common Problems

⁊ℓ

Depression

The word 'depression' is used to cover a lot of states, ranging from a mild feeling of the blues to a severe medical condition. It is often an insidious process, so that even the person concerned, and his or her family, may be unaware of what is happening. The sooner it is identified the better, as it is best to treat it as early as possible.

It usually starts with a general state of chronic fatigue, a loss of vitality and interest, and the feeling that everything has become a burden. It can manifest itself through anxiety, which may be caused by real or unreal situations but is most often quite unfounded. Then phobias can develop, as fear and irrational behaviour gradually take over a person's life.

Bereavement, divorce, relationship problems, unemployment and serious illness can all lead to depression. Insomnia and too much stress can also be the cause. And when the endocrine system is not functioning properly, as in premenstrual tension, the menopause, and sometimes after childbirth, a depressive state can develop all too easily.

We can all suffer from low spirits from time to time. It is only when mood becomes so low that it impairs the quality and normality of life that it becomes serious, and severe cases of depression need to be treated medically.

HOW AROMATHERAPY CAN HELP

A good aromatherapist can help a person suffering from occasional bouts of depression by encouraging her to adopt a positive attitude to life and by using aromatic products.

Whether her depression is a recent development or of longer standing, we give a stimulating massage using a slightly faster rhythm than usual to give an uplift. Fortifying essential oils, such as bay, juniper, geranium, lavender, rose, jasmine and ylang ylang are used.

The depressed person may gain great relief simply by discussing her worries with the therapist. She may start to cry, especially when the solar plexus, an important centre of the body's nerve crossings and magnetism, is massaged. Crying is a beneficial way of expressing those inner emotions that are all too often suppressed, causing a great deal of misery.

The therapist can help a lot by encouraging the client to assess her way of life and consider what self-help may be possible. Depressed people often refrain from socializing and lose interest in other people, so we may try to encourage her to get involved with others, perhaps by helping them in some way.

The depressed client usually looks forward to visiting the therapist, often because the latter is the only person who is prepared to listen. Depressive people tend to have a negative outlook on life and people generally avoid spending time with them. In order to keep a client on an even keel, we will probably advise a weekly treatment.

HOME CARE

We also work out a programme of home care that the client can follow on her own and will suggest body and bath oils that will help lift the mood.

It is important to follow a good diet. Experiments have shown that balanced nutrition can do a great deal to reduce unruly or irrational behaviour. Even quite serious mental and emotional imbalances can be helped by the right diet with a plentiful supply of vitamins and minerals. Wholesome food, with plenty of fresh fruit and vegetables, will not only improve a person's appearance, but also helps to return her life to a state of harmony.

Alcohol should be avoided or taken only in very small amounts, as any feeling of uplift in mood is quickly followed by a corresponding drop. This is a time when it can be all too easy to look for some kind of prop and to become dependent on drink or drugs.

It is a good idea to drink at least one cup of herb tea a day. The following are all very good for helping depression: camomile, hawthorn, lavender, lime blossom, marjoram, melissa, mint, sage, thyme and lemon verbena.

Regular exercise and plenty of fresh air will improve a person's general state of health. Yoga exercises are particularly good, working not only on the body but also having a good influence on mental and emotional levels. Any pleasant recreation, such as reading and listening to cheerful music, can also be beneficial.

ALLERGIES

Allergies can cause all sorts of reactions, and can actually aggravate depression. If they occur on the skin they are relatively easy to diagnose, but sometimes symptoms can be vague and difficult to pinpoint.

If it seems possible that a food or drink may be the cause, it is advisable to try to find the culprit. I find the best way of doing this is to eliminate the suspected food for one week, and to monitor the results. Carry on in this way until the allergy has been identified.

SEVERE DEPRESSION

Unfortunately there are severe cases of depression that can take years of drugs and psychotherapy to overcome. When a client is suffering from a severe condition of this kind, our role is still to be supportive, but progress is likely to be slow, and the therapist needs a lot of patience and understanding. We use all the resources we can muster in order to be positive and to counteract the low and negative state of mind of the client.

Strong essential oils such as bay, geranium, incense, lavender, rosemary and ylang ylang are used and the massage is slightly faster than usual. Smell can have a powerful, uplifting influence on the client and we find that we always get some improvement, however slight. We also use essential oils on a fragrancer in the treatment room in order to give a lift to the atmosphere.

Sometimes the client may be heavily drugged and unable to take in everything the therapist advises, but perseverance will, in the long run, work.

Fortunately, we see very few clients in such a condition. When we think a client needs medical help, we refer her either back to her own doctor or to a homeopathic doctor.

The Common Cold

There are several simple measures that you can take both to prevent and to treat colds.

PREVENTION

When the cold season starts in the autumn, we advise our clients to start using products to protect them against the cold virus. We particularly recommend using a fragrancer and diffusing the essential oils of cajuput, eucalyptus, niaouli, pine and thyme on it. Use them individually, or two or three of them mixed together. They will ensure a highly antiseptic atmosphere.

Another thing you can do if you feel a cold threatening is to put a drop of niaouli on a tissue, and to inhale it occasionally. This clears the nasal passages. Be careful, however, not to place the essential oil directly on the nose as it may cause irritation to the skin.

At night, take a bath with six drops of one of the highly antiseptic essential oils known to be good for colds. These include cajuput, eucalyptus, niaouli and pine.

Lastly, do not forget to take regular doses of vitamin C. This is helpful in reinforcing the immune system.

WHEN A COLD DEVELOPS

Use a fragrancer with the essential oils mentioned above. It is a good idea to drink a cup of hot, boiled water every three hours to cleanse the system. Three times a day, drink a cup of thyme herb tea to which you have added the juice of half a lemon and a teaspoon of honey to fight the infection.

Prepare a bath with the essential oils mentioned above and soak in it for 10 to 15 minutes. The bath should be hot enough to induce perspiration but remember that very hot baths are not recommended for people with cardiovascular problems, high blood pressure and varicose veins, nor for pregnant women.

After your bath, wrap yourself in a towelling robe and sweat it out for as long as you like, but when you start to feel chilly you should change into warm clothes. This is excellent for getting rid of toxins. Then go to bed.

Take one aromatic bath a day for three days, then return to the usual recommended practice of taking four aromatic baths a week.

Eat a light diet as long as you have no temperature. If you have a fever, take only liquids.

Inhale niaouli as outlined above. If your chest is affected, apply an oil made of 2 per cent essential oils of niaouli, eucalyptus and pine in wheatgerm vegetable oil to your chest, morning and night.

Rest is very important to give your system the chance to fight the infection, so stay in bed as much as you can.

Problems of the Digestive Tract

People who do not digest their food well tend to get bloated, to suffer from an excess of acidity and sometimes to have pains in the stomach. When a client tells us that she suffers from problems of the digestive tract, the first thing we do is to check her diet, and also the way in which she eats.

FOOD COMBINING

Often it is the combination of foods that is to blame rather than any individual foods. Some food combinations can be very unhealthy, causing acidity, flatulence and discomfort.

For many years now we have recommended the method of food combining pioneered by Dr William Howard Hay over 50 years ago. The Hay system, as it has come to be known, advises not mixing carbohydrates and proteins at the same meal. The body uses acids to digest proteins and alkalis to digest carbohydrates, and mixing the two in the same meal can lead to poor digestion.

EATING HABITS

We also check the way in which the client eats. It is important to chew food well, to eat slowly and to eat in pleasant, harmonious conditions. When asked, 90 per cent of our clients say that they tend to eat too fast, in a hurry, while talking, and in noisy conditions.

Our experience has shown that many minor digestive problems can be attributed to these bad habits.

How Aromatherapy Can Help

Massage, first of all, is very useful. The therapist works particularly on the digestive reflex zones of the back to stimulate and regulate the digestive tract. The massage preparations contain essential oils such as basil, camomile, marjoram, peppermint and thyme, all of which have a beneficial action on the digestive tract.

We recommend our clients to refrain from drinking with meals, which tends to bloat the stomach. We also recommend that they drink herb teas such as camomile, basil, peppermint, marjoram and thyme, which should be drunk after meals.

We usually find that small digestive 'miseries' go away on this regime. When we find, however, that the problem is too deep or that there is no improvement, we suggest that our client consults her doctor for diagnosis and further advice.

Emotional Upsets

Digestive problems are sometimes caused by emotional upsets. In this case, the therapist combines the use of relaxing essential oils, such as lavender and vetivert, with ones that act on the digestive tract, such as camomile, marjoram and peppermint. This combined treatment should help to restore a client's balance until her emotional problem has been solved.

For home treatment, we recommend body and bath oils that are good for the digestive tract, using the same essential oils as in the clinic.

Aches and Pains

Aches and pains cover a multitude of problems. They can be caused by an excessive amount of exercise, gardening, injuries, rheumatism, arthritis, stress, or they can, quite simply, be the result of a bout of influenza. They can be temporary, or they can be chronic.

Whatever the cause, treatment with essential oils is most helpful for improving blood circulation and for relieving blockages and fluid infiltrations affecting muscles or joints. Muscle spasms and contractions can cause a lot of pain, in which case the massage is very soothing, decontracting and brings quick relief.

Essential Oils

We use a variety of different essential oils, depending on the exact nature of the condition. Sage is good for its action on the endocrine system and for fluid retention; lavender for its decontracting effect, which is particularly beneficial in case of spasm, and its soothing effect on the nervous system; rosemary for its decongestive action; and thyme for its antiseptic qualities, which help improve the condition of the joints. Sometimes we use the essential oil required singly, sometimes we mix two or three together. Either way, we use 4 per cent of essential oil mixed with a vegetable oil, which is usually wheatgerm or St John's wort.

HOME CARE

We suggest that our client uses a specific body oil and bath product, based on the essential oils recommended above. If any area is particularly inflamed and painful, we recommend warm compresses, plus one drop only of essential oil of sage or lavender put on the compress. Remove the compress when it starts to get cold. Repeat this twice a day until the pain eases.

Warm poultices of crushed linseed can also bring relief, and should again be removed when they start to get cold. A leaf of Savoy cabbage, well washed and flattened with a rolling pin, can be highly beneficial on a problem area. Leave for at least an hour.

ONE WOMAN'S EXPERIENCE . . .

Rosemary Burr first hobbled into Micheline Arcier's clinic nearly ten years ago. Her leg was in plaster with her toes badly bruised and her body ached all over. It had been suggested to her that aromatherapy would help reduce her bruising and generally lift her spirits and give her a sense of wellbeing.

All this was proved right and the feeling of relaxation that followed her treatment was a great antidote to the aches and pains caused by her broken leg. The colour returned to her cheeks, the knots were tweaked out of her neck and she felt totally at ease. Even though the plaster cast is now a thing of the past, she still makes regular visits.

She recaptures her experiences in the clinic at home using bath oils which produce a delightfully scented reminder of her treatments.

The Family

Child Care

Like adults, children live in a highly polluted and stressful environment and aromatherapy can help maintain good health and a strong immune system. The dosage of essential oils in products for children is much lower than that used for adults. It depends not only on the severity of the condition but on the size and age of a child and the potency of the essence.

EARLY BABYHOOD

A baby's skin is highly sensitive to touch, and is often dry, sometimes with a tendency to eczema.

Many of our clients ask us to prepare an oil for the newborn baby and, unless there is a definite medical problem, we make up an oil that can be used on both the face and body. We use one drop only of essential oil of Roman camomile mixed with 100 ml (4 fl oz) of almond vegetable oil. The essential oil should give off only very faint odour. This oil can be used every time the baby is bathed, and is particularly useful for cleaning the top of the head, which has a tendency to be crusty. We advise the mothers to massage the oil gently and soothingly into the baby's skin. Pressure should not be applied, especially on the top of the head where the fragile fontanelle is.

If the baby has eczema, we make a special oil with Roman camomile, neroli or sandalwood in St John's wort vegetable oil. A diet devoid of dairy produce and, later on, meat is advisable, but it is best to take medical advice.

When you change the baby's nappy, spray the baby's bottom with a little Evian water after washing. This is very alkaline and therefore highly beneficial, since nappy rash is usually caused by soreness due to the acidity of the urine and stools. Let it dry and follow with either a little oil or some clay powder (rather than talcum powder), which is highly antiseptic and contains no harmful chemical elements.

BATH TIME

A morning bath is usually better when the baby is very young. Essential oils are too strong to use in a baby's bath up to the age of two years. We recommend rather a decoction of camomile. You can make this by putting 5 to 10 heads of Roman camomile flowers (depending on the size of the bath) in a pan with 300 ml (½ pt) of water. Boil for 10 minutes, strain and mix with the bath water.

It is not, in any case, advisable to put pure essential oils in the bath for children. They do not mix with the water but stay on the surface, where they can irritate the child's eyes and skin.

The baby's eyes can be cleaned with a little cooled boiled water or mineral water. Alternatively, you can make up some fresh camomile lotion by pouring 150 ml (¼ pt) of boiling water on to one camomile flower; infuse for 10 minutes, strain and allow to cool.

After his bath, particularly if he is not sleeping well, it helps to give a soothing massage with a little oil. Five minutes is enough and will pacify a restless baby.

The Baby's Room

The baby's bedroom will benefit from an electric fragrancer with a few drops of essential oil of eucalyptus or niaouli to disinfect the atmosphere. Do not leave the essential oil to dry – put it on the fragrancer for a maximum of one or two hours, then switch off.

If the baby's room is centrally heated, a humidifier will keep the air healthy for the baby's respiratory tract. If you live in a highly polluted area, it may be wise to invest in an ionizer.

If the baby's nose is slightly congested, put one drop of essential oil of cajuput or niaouli on a handkerchief and suspend it on the side of the cot, out of the baby's reach.

It is most important to surround a baby with a world of light, refreshing, uplifting smells. These have a great effect, from a very early age, on the formation of a sense of smell.

To calm a baby who is difficult to settle, try giving him a weak camomile tea, either on its own or mixed with orange juice. Rocking the baby and putting him against his mother's heart will help to relax him. It will remind him of the peaceful time he spent inside his mother's womb, with the reassuring sound of her heartbeat.

Prickly heat can be very uncomfortable and causes a lot of distress. Evian spray will help with this. Put him in pure cotton garments only.

The Toddler

When the baby is older, night-time baths are better. We have a range of bath products, including highly antiseptic essential oils such as cajuput, eucalyptus, niaouli and tangerine (for its vitamin content); juniper (fortify-ing); and camomile, lavender and neroli (for their calming effect and to take care of dry, sensitive skin). It is wise to buy a bath product that is already mixed with an element that allows the essential oil to be dispersed in the water, otherwise the pure essential oil will stay on the surface of the water and can cause irritation.

We suggest a very weak Dermarome solution for cuts, bruises and burns.

The area can be sponged with this solution, as it is quite antiseptic.

We have seen children with growing difficulties show great improvement when a body oil made up of essential oil of tangerine in soya vegetable oil is massaged onto their body every day after the bath. The exact percentage depends on the child.

Fragrancers are useful for colds and respiratory tract infections.

School Days

When the child starts nursery school, this is the time when he mixes with many other children and is likely to catch all kinds of infection. We recommend body oils, which are both easy and enjoyable for a child to use. Children are surprisingly good at applying them, provided you involve them and explain exactly why they are such a good idea. They also enjoy doing everything that they have seen their parents do.

Essential oils of cajuput, eucalyptus and niaouli help combat colds; lavender, marjoram and neroli are relaxing; and juniper, lavender, orange and tangerine are fortifying.

Early Skin Care

A good routine of skin care is advisable from an early age. Some children are already affected by dry skin, and the tendency to have spots is not that far off for many of them. A face oil made up of essential oils of camomile and sandalwood in sesame vegetable oil is very useful. Again the percentage depends on the individual.

In our consulting rooms, we occasionally see clients as young as nine having a skin care treatment. Their mothers often feel that we are better at training them and at explaining why it is important, and we have even advised young boys with skin problems.

We show them a simple routine of cleansing, and explain the importance of diet. We recommend them to use a clay mask at least once a week, and show them how to protect sensitive skins with a light film of oil. With the onset of puberty, we sometimes have to deal with acne (see pages 109–10).

Men

Many of our lady clients buy products for their partners, and we also have many male customers who buy our products. Men benefit from face and body products just as much as women do, and to this end we have a special range for men.

Skin Care

Like women, men can suffer from many different skin conditions. In recent years, we have seen a great increase in the number of men taking better care of themselves and their appearance, and skin care is no longer considered to be an exclusively feminine concern.

Face oil A face oil, to be smoothed on to the face, can be used instead of aftershave lotion, and has the added advantage that it not only protects and soothes the skin but also improves and nourishes it. Alternatively, the following formulations may come in useful.

Sensitive and congested skin 2 per cent essential oils of lavender and sandalwood in sesame, wheatgerm or grapeseed vegetable oil.

Oily skin 3 per cent essential oils of bay and lemon in soya or grapeseed vegetable oil.

Acneic skin 3 per cent essential oils of juniper and lemon in sesame or soya vegetable oil.

Dehydrated, lined and prematurely aged skin 3 per cent essential oils of patchouli, sandalwood and ylang ylang in grapeseed or wheatgerm vegetable oil.

Normal skin 3 per cent essential oils of basil, lavender and ylang ylang in grapeseed or sesame vegetable oil.

BODY AND BATH OILS

Our standard range of body and bath products can be used successfully for men as well as women. However, special formulations of body oils can be made up specifically for men, using 4 per cent essential oils of any of the following: bay, basil, cypress, geranium, lemon, lavender, niaouli, pine, sage, sandalwood, vetivert or ylang ylang, in either sesame, soya or grapeseed vegetable oil. The body oils can be used either on their own, morning or night, or after an aromatic bath.

Useful Addresses

Micheline Arcier Aromatherapy
7 William Street, London, SW1X 9HL
Tel: 071-235 3545
For aromatic face, body and bath oils, pure essences, fragrancers and treatments. Mail order available.

Dr Renaud Skin Care
Head office - 92 Rue de la Victoire, 75009
Paris, France
UK distributor - 2 Roman Road, Storeton Village,
The Wirral, L63 6HS
US distributor - 20 Marion Street,
Plattsburg, New York 12901, US
For natural masks and cleansing milks

Pierre Cattier SA
Head Office - 33 Rue Maurice Marion,
91270 Vigneux, France
UK distributor - Mayflower Beauty Products,
Island Farm Avenue, Molesey Trading
Estate, East Molesey, Surrey, KT8 0UZ
Tel: 081-979 7261
For Pierre Cattier clay products

Dr Valnet's Seaweed Baths
Head Office - Laboratoire Cosbionat,
22 Rue Villebois-Mareuil, 92230
Gennevilliers, Paris
UK distributor - Cedar Health Ltd,
Pepper Road, Hazel Grove, Stockport, SK7 5BW
Tel: 061-483 1235

Cantassuim Vitamins and Minerals
Tel: 081-874 1130
For natural vitamins and minerals

Biocosmetics Ltd
distributed by Power Health
Products Ltd, 10 Central Avenue,
Airfield Estate, Pocklington,
York, YO4 2NR
For vegetable oils

International Federation of
Aromatherapists
Dept of Continuing Education,
The Royal Masonic Hospital,
Ravenscourt Park, London W6 0TN
The official body representing the interests of aromatherapists and ensuring high standards of training and work. Please enclose s.a.e. with enquiry.

British Association of Beauty Therapy and
Cosmetology
2nd Floor, 34 Imperial Square, Cheltenham,
Gloucestershire, GL50 1QZ
Write for a list of recognized schools and colleges for training in massage and beauty therapy. Enclose s.a.e. for details.

Northern Institute of Massage
100 Waterloo Road, Blackpool, FY4 1AW

British Homeopathic Association
27a Devonshire Street, London, W1N 1RJ
Send s.a.e. for list of homeopathic doctors in and around your area, plus general information on homeopathy

The National Center for Homeopathy
1500 Massachusetts Avenue Northwest, Suite
42 Washington DC 20005, US

Foresight
28 The Paddock
Godalming, Surrey, GU7 1XD
Tel: 0483-427839
The Association for the promotion of preconceptual care

Weight Watchers (UK)
Kidwells Park House, Kidwells Park Drive,
Maidenhead, Berkshire, SL6 8YT
Tel: 0628 777077

Training Courses
I have been training students from all over the world for many years now. As I specialize in aromatherapy I therefore train only people who are already qualified in face and body massage, anatomy and physiology.

My experience has taught me that it is often the more mature and experienced person who stands the best chance of success as an aromatherapist. As well as skill and knowledge of the subject, the holistic approach of aromatherapy means that it requires a great understanding of human nature.

I recommend my students to join the Federation of Aromatherapists, which was founded a few years ago. It is most important that we have an official body representing the interests of aromatherapists while, at the same time, ensuring a high standard of work and training.

Index